FORTUNE COOKIE

crack open to understand and grow

LEADERSHIP

Wisdom for Leadership, Sales & Life

KATEY DALLOSTO

Wendy—
Make It
Happen!

Grazie!
Katey

www.CapisceConsulting.com

Fortune Cookie Leadership: Wisdom for Leadership, Sales & Life
© 2017 Katey Dallosto

Published through Capisce Publishing in collaboration with Electric Moon Publishing, LLC an author-friendly, custom publishing place.
www.emoonpublishing.com
info@emoonpublishing.com

E-book
    ISBN-10: 1-943027-16-1
    ISBN-13: 978-1-943027-16-3
Paperback
    ISBN-10: 1-943027-15-3
    ISBN-13: 978-1-943027-15-6

Cover Design: Alyssa Busse and Lyn Rayn, Electric Moon Publishing Creative Art Department
Interior Design: Lyn Rayn, Electric Moon Publishing Creative Art Department

Capisce Consulting
Understand & Grow

High Trust Selling relies on transparent and honest conversations. Katey's simple yet powerful "fortune cookie" wisdom will aid in getting those conversations started. Combining her personal, revealing and fun style with a little tough love, Katey will help you build more high trust as she leads you to greater success in your sales and leadership.

-Todd Duncan, *New York Times* best-selling author,
High Trust Selling and Time Traps

Fortune Cookie Leadership flat out delivers! You are holding a leadership playbook that is going to inspire you, motivate you, and serve as your go-to tool for the days you need a boost. The book is not just about how to be an effective leader, it is really a roadmap to how to live an amazing life regardless of your age, title, or career path. I am planning on giving copies to all my close friends so that they can use it to elevate their results and happiness! If you put this book down you will miss out on a remarkable tool! Choose wisely and jump in!

-Jonathan Roche, award-winning fitness expert, 12-time Ironman
Triathlon finisher, 22-time Boston Marathon finisher and best-selling
author of *The No Excuses Diet that hit #3 on the Amazon best seller list*

Katey Dallosto is a special spirit—optimistic, energetic, and wise. She is a magnetic speaker and teacher, with lots of pizzazz. Now she has written a book that epitomizes her wonderful style. *Fortune Cookie Leadership* is fun to read, uplifting, and full of inspirational morsels. Katey, and her fortune cookies, don't waste words. They deliver with perspective and punch! Katey had dedicated herself to guiding others toward a fuller life and more effective leadership. This book is the latest evidence of her dedication. Read it and leap!

-Dave Jenks, national speaker, and co-author of *New York Times*
best-selling titles *The Millionaire Real Estate Agent*,
The Millionaire Real Estate Investor and Shift.

Katey dedicated *Fortune Cookie Leadership* to her mother, Ann Carr Dallosto—a loyal colleague, wise mentor, and friend of mine. Ann possessed a remarkable ability to discover connections between individuals, instantly transforming strangers into friends. Relationships ruled with Ann and when faced with problems or challenges, she prayed, discerned, and delivered prudent and pragmatic solutions. Katey shares the wisdom and charisma of her mother within the pages of *Fortune Cookie Leadership*, and I encourage you to read each nugget of counsel with a teachable heart.

-Carol Swain, Professor and Vice President of
Mission, Saint Mary's College of Moraga

Katey presents fifty-two common-sense "devotions" on sales, leadership, and life using astute observations, shrewd intellect, and humor to boot. Reminded me of my Dad's remark when I told him "That's a fairly large goal, Dad." Dad's response: "That's no hill for a climber!" *Fortune Cookie Leadership* is a tremendous read for any and all, especially for those climbing high in the leadership and sales industry!

-Doug Long, EVP, HomeBridge Financial Services

Top sales trainer and coach Katey Dallosto offers valuable leadership, life, and sales takeaways in her title *Fortune Cookie Leadership*. Katey's depth of experience has led her to share fifty-two quick pieces of wisdom that will give the reader encouragement, ensure laughter, and definitely impart energy to reach career and life goals!

-Gene Frederick, Board of Directors, EXP Holdings, Inc.,
Author, *101 Ways to Lead Generate in Real Estate*

Katey Dallosto's *Fortune Cookie Leadership* is powerful! Katey gives countless examples of skills we already possess, but have never tapped into, and inspires us to use these skills to build stronger, more lucrative businesses and get more joy out of life! Open the BEST Fortune Cookie of your life and read this book!

-Mary Ann Benedetti, former top performing *Weight Watchers* leader

CONTENTS

FOREWORD

Fortune Cookie Leadership is a tribute to my parents, my sister, my children, my love, Chuck, and to keeping it simple. The origins of the book can be attributed to my mother, Ann Carr Dallosto, who passed away in 1998 at the way too early age of 55. She was not only a teacher, but a teacher of teachers at St. Mary's College in Moraga, California. Mom tended to parent with many of one-liners you will find in this book. Those same one-liners continue to guide me, my sister, and hundreds of teachers today.

My oldest daughter, Kelsey, once noticed that I use a lot of "one-liners" in my own parenting. After using one of them one day, she smiled and said, "You sound like a fortune cookie." The nickname and the inspiration for the book was born!

I soon realized that my use of these one liners was not restricted to my home-life. While managing large real estate offices from 2006 to 2012, I realized that my most effective moments were in my weekly sales meetings. I formatted each meeting with a training component designed to influence and benefit those sales associates who chose to attend. To encourage their attendance, I needed to create value for them in each meeting. One of the challenges I faced was finding some sort of theme or focus for the week. I would spend countless hours researching video clips, articles, and websites to find an impactful theme that would connect with the agents. Many times I ultimately defaulted to the wisdoms that my own mom shared with me.

As I spoke with my counterparts at other companies, I quickly learned I was not the only one who faced the challenge of creating content of value. Most recently, while working for a large mortgage company as a sales and leadership consultant. Throughout my territory, I continued to see similar struggles to find powerful yet simple messages to inspire and motivate salespeople, particularly independent contractors.

As I continued to train, do speaking events, and even one-on-one consulting, it became very apparent that these same one-liners my mom shared with me and I shared with my children had a similar impact when I shared them with my business associates. They seemed to be touched in a simple yet powerful way. When I began to hear these words and one-liners being repeated by people whom I had shared them, and see the impact they were having on their lives and business, I knew I needed to collect them in a form that I could share with a broader audience. So the idea for this book began.

Each brief chapter of this book is simply the tip of the iceberg. They are designed to inspire, motivate, and generate a much lengthier and deeper discussion on each topic. In some cases, volumes of books have already been written. For almost all the chapters, I have presented hours of materials and am willing to do so again if you would like to contact me.

My consulting company is *Capisce Consulting: Understand and Grow*. When translated, "capisce" means "Got it?" or "Understand?" I truly believe when we strive to understand each other we can grow together.

Capisce is not the only Italian word you will see within these pages. As you read the book, you may notice the light use of the Italian language. My mother was 100% Irish and my father is 100% Italian. My mom wanted to make sure people knew I was Irish, so my first name is Katey, with an Irish spelling. Dallosto, on the other hand, is a Northern Italian name. Physically, I look Italian, except for my "Irish eyes." As a college student, I spent a summer abroad in Assisi, Italy and fell in love. I fell in love with the Italian language, the people, the culture, the art, and of course the food! Upon my return to Santa Clara University, I decided to major in marketing and minor in Italian. My ultimate goal is to speak the language fluently and live in Italy for a month each year. My kids have gotten used to me pulling from my Italian phrases as I parent so I hope you will indulge me too as you read along.

No matter the language, my ultimate goal is that these simple, yet powerful one-liners will not only help and inspire the individual salesperson who is looking to grow his or her business, but will also aid the branch or sales manager who is looking to motivate his or her team or add additional value to meetings. I want to wish you all the very best and much success. Happy selling.

Capisce?

PREFACE

HOW TO USE THIS BOOK

You have this book in your hands . . . Now what? The intention of the book is 52 weeks of inspiration for you and your sales team. If you are an entrepreneur, it may help get you closer to your goals. If you are a sales leader there is now content and inspiration for you and your team for 52 weeks of the year.

How to use this book:

- Read the book cover to cover
- Flip through the book and see what strikes you this week
- Use one chapter to inspire more research on a particular topic
- Plan out focus or inspiration for the month, quarter or year
- For additional sales leadership support contact www.CapisceConsulting.com

Hopefully you and your team will find this a helpful tool.

Here is to your success!
Katey

Katey Dallosto
Owner, Speaker & Coach
www.CapisceConsulting.com

ACKNOWLEDGMENTS

Today, I am thinking of my dear friend, Nate Ellis, and all the pictures in my mind of the memories we shared. Nate died at the early age of thirty-nine after a long-fought battle with a debilitating disease. He is now at peace. Nate was my employee, my friend, my co-conspirator, my vision caster, my inspiration, and my kick in the pants. Nate and I both had a passion for training, coaching, and public speaking. With so many people having such a strong fear about public speaking, it is often difficult to get constructive feedback after doing it. Nate and I helped each other to improve our skills as trainers and speakers. I always treasured his opinion, and his feedback was invaluable.

Nate and I also shared a passion for listening to other speakers and trainers. We read many of the same books, went to events together, and shared our thoughts on these events. Nate and I started to help each other stay focused on the positive images we wanted for ourselves. Words, along with images, have power.

Nate was a true inspiration and wonderful human being. He loved to sing and was often known for breaking out into a rendition of "Danke Shoen" at any given moment. I loved to meet up with him after his travels to learn from him and share in his enthusiasm in living his passion. We often joked that someday we would be high-fiving each other as one took the stage after the other.

When Nate's illness made it too difficult to continue with travel, he was already known as one of the best trainers of the National Association of REALTOR®. Nate achieved his goal. Unfortunately, his illness took his life.

Nate achieved so much in his short time on this earth and touched so many lives. He had a knack for staying positive while continuing to focus on his goals and vision for success.

Even after his death, Nate is held in high regard. A national real estate award "The Nate Ellis Giving Back Award" was established in his honor. I was privileged to be there the night the first award was given to our mutual friend and mentor, Jim Walberg.

Nate's memory and legacy continue. Even though Nate is in heaven, released from his physical suffering, I continue to grieve the loss of my friend. I have promised to make Nate proud and to continue the vision that we had set out to achieve. As I continue to speak and train, I will be taking a moment before each event to high-five Nate in a special way in my heart. I love you, Nate!

CLOSED MOUTHS DON'T GET FED!

This is the most simple and obvious thing in sales. You must ask for the business. No one is a mind reader. It is amazing to me how many salespeople spend so much time developing a relationship and then forget to ask for the business. Everyone knows you are running a business. They expect you to offer your product or service, particularly in a sales meeting, so do it! Of course, the best sales video on this subject is Blake, the Alec Baldwin character in the movie, *Glengarry Glen Ross*, with his "ABC" mantra. ABC stands for "Always Be Closing!"[1]

I was trained in a high pressure, high results focused, outside sales environment. Part of our training involved how to close throughout the entire sales presentation. Ask for *buy-in* at the outset of the meeting. Ask for clarification on needs. Ask for clarification on objections. The basic time format for a great sales presentation is as follows:

- Build rapport (20%)
- Perform need analysis (40%)
- Present solutions (20%)
- Handle objections (15%)
- Close for next steps (5%)

When a prospective client or referral partner meets with you, part of his or her expectation is to learn about your business. It is a safe place to ask for what you need. If you need referrals to grow your business, then ask! If you are looking to add valuable team members, then ask! If you are looking for Yelp reviews, then ask! If you need feedback on your latest advertising/sales presentation/website, then ask!

Americans are the creators of Superman and Wonder Woman. Everyone loves to be a superhero. When someone asks you to help him or her, and you can actually do so, doesn't it feel good? Your past clients, as well as your new clients and associates, will also feel good to help you, too. Don't be afraid to let everyone know what you do and how well you do it! Your actions, tied with your words, are powerful. Passion and enthusiasm sell. So open your mouth and get fed!

TELL ME WHO YOUR FRIENDS ARE AND I WILL TELL YOU WHO YOU WANT TO BE

2

LEADERSHIP

My sister, Karolyn, and I would often comment that Mom was part "witch." She had this uncanny intuition that helped her see people in ways they couldn't see themselves. I am lucky to have developed some of this gift as well, though nowhere near as well as Mom. When we would bring friends over to the house, Mom was very discerning about who we called our friends. One of her favorite lines was, "Tell me who your friends are and I will tell you who you want to be." She would remind us that our associates can either help drive us to be better or pull us down to their level. Eagles fly with eagles!

Associates, friends, colleagues, and even companies can tell you who you want to be. Are you surrounding yourself with people that connect and support your vision, goals, and core values? Or do they sabotage, undermine, and criticize them? Are the people around you anchors or sails?

A few years after my divorce, I had put on quite a bit of weight and wasn't happy. I decided I needed to lose thirty-five pounds. During this process, I gave up alcohol. This was difficult because I love sports and enjoy watching games with my friends at a sports bar. I'd show up to the bar with my buddies and was instantly told how great I looked. The congratulatory banter was really nice and supportive.

Immediately after sitting down during one such occasion, one of my friends teased me for not having a beer. I shot back, "You cannot congratulate me on looking great then make fun of me for not having a beer!" It was in that moment that I decided I need to be very careful who I surrounded myself with during this process. It turned into an opportunity to look at all of my relationships, both personal and professional. I became very particular about the people with whom I spent time on a regular basis. It turned out that in the process, I did lose a few friends and thirty-five pounds!

In the three years following my divorce, I went from renting a post-divorce crappy apartment, being overweight, having way too much credit card debt, and being in unhealthy relationships, to buying a new house on my own, being a healthy weight, and creating healthy relationships, including falling in love with Chuck. It was interesting to watch my "friends" change as I became a better version of myself.

I have always had this image of myself as one of the prisoners as depicted in Michelangelo's unfinished sculptures known as "The Prisoners." They are unfinished marble sculptures. Michelangelo was known to have said that he was just releasing the masterpiece hidden beneath the marble. His job was just to chip away the excess to bring out the masterpiece hidden beneath. Going through my post-divorce transformation helped me learn how to be released from the excess marble that was keeping me a prisoner. The company we keep helps us become the masterpiece we are meant to be. When I look at clients, I want to help them be released from whatever sort of marble is hiding the potential within them or their company.

Are your friends and associates helping you to become the best part of yourself? Are they your biggest fans? Are you theirs? Who supports you in going out for a healthy walk instead of cocktails and happy hour? Who challenges you to do your daily activities to meet your weekly, monthly, and annual goals?

If among your friends and colleagues, you are the smartest, best looking, most prayerful, most healthy, and find that most everyone agrees with you, then YOU NEED NEW FRIENDS!

It is better to be the dumbest kid in MENSA than the smartest kid among underachievers.

Iron sharpens iron.

Be around people who sharpen and challenge you in every aspect of your life.

Tell me who your friends are and I will tell you who you want to be.

NOTES

IF YOU DON'T WANT ANYONE TO KNOW IT, THEN DON'T DO IT

Ahhh, this was one of my mother's favorites. There were many times in my adult life that listening to this advice would have served me well. This lesson is really all about open, honest, and transparent communication. You might as well start off by telling the truth. The truth always comes out, usually when you least expect it. As politicians and celebrities find, the cover-up is often worse than the act itself.

During my career in real estate, I attended quite a few legal seminars. Real estate is a very litigious industry. REALTOR® are often held to some challenging legal standards, including "what you should know" about a property. My favorite legal advice for being open, honest, and transparent is simply, "Begin every email, text, or conversation in your head with 'ladies and gentlemen of the jury' and you will be fine." Every email, letter, or text can be read in open court. Sometimes tensions and emotions run hot and can get the better of us. Take a moment before you hit the send key and ask yourself, "Would I want this read in open court?"

Those who work in sales will have many opportunities to work in the "grey area" to close the deal. It can be especially tempting when a high percentage of your compensation is based on closed transactions. As leaders, we need to remind our teams that cutting a corner for one transaction can ruin a career. Is it worth it? Do you think no one will find out about it? If your core values include honesty and transparency, then the path becomes clear. It is easier to clean up a mess of honesty than to walk through a land mine of misinformation, omissions, and lies.

As kids, we used to watch *Little House on the Prairie* with Mom. In Walnut Grove, the small town setting for the show, everyone seemed to know what was happening in everyone else's household. This knowledge created a sense of community, support, and moral validation. Most of the town went to school, the market, and church together. They had few secrets. In today's shrinking world of the internet, social media, and cameras everywhere, we are living in our own global Walnut Grove. We don't have many secrets. So, why do we need them?

Facebook, Twitter, Snapchat, Instagram, etc., are all opportunities to remind us that if you don't want anyone to know it, then don't do it! I remind my friends that anything posted to my Facebook page is visible to my boss, my priest, my children, and my dad. My greatest fear is when I receive a message saying I've been tagged in a post by a friend of over thirty years. What decade and activity is that picture going to reflect? I have had times in my life when I did not adhere to my mother's advice. It is a reminder to make better choices. As the great Maya Angelou once said, "When we know better, we do better.[1]"

The idea of privacy has always made me laugh. Yes, some family decisions and issues need to be discussed within the family. But there is a difference between privacy and secrets. Privacy is determining the appropriate level of intimate sharing and conversation with the appropriate people. Secrecy usually begins with, "Don't tell anyone . . ."

According to Brené Brown, "Shame hates it when we reach out and tell our story. It hates having words wrapped around it—it can't survive being shared. Shame loves secrecy. When we bury our story, the shame metastasizes."[2]

Shame hates the light! We are human. We make mistakes. We make bad choices. The key to success is to get up, own it, ask for forgiveness, and move forward. I consider my life like a patchwork quilt: it contains lots of different colors, patterns, and shapes. Some pieces of my quilt are not pretty and not the best part of me. Those pieces provide the contrast that brings out the beautiful colors and vibrancy of the quilt of my life. I am grateful for those moments of falling down, of having the opportunity to connect with people at a deeply vulnerable level, to challenge my faith and to refocus on who I am at my core. Those moments may not be my proudest moments, yet they led me to a better path that I am proud to share with anyone.

NOTES

TWO EARS . . . ONE MOUTH

This is one of those "self-talk" lessons. Whenever I say this, it is a reminder of what I need to <u>do</u> more . . . *listen*. God gave us two ears and one mouth. Let's use them in the appropriate proportion.

My friend and mentor, Todd Duncan, demonstrates this during his High Trust Sales Academy. Most salespeople fall into the trap of talking too much when doing a sales presentation. Todd asks the participants of his academy to "sell your neighbor your pen." Since salespeople are typically enthusiastic and competitive, they are ready to win. The students in the academy all begin by telling their neighbor all the great reasons why this pen is amazing: color, comfort, clip, ease of use, weight, size, etc. The "customer" often just sits there while the salesperson does a "feature vomit" all over them. Most customers barely get a word in during the entire exercise. Many of the salespeople will close with, "So, do you want to buy the pen?"

They forget that they have two ears and one mouth. We all want others to think we are smart, so we end up telling people everything we know. However, often the best sales presentations are done when the salesperson does the *least* amount of talking. Try to adhere to the Abraham Lincoln quote: "It is better to keep your mouth shut and be thought a fool than to open it and remove all doubt."

As a fan of the TV show *Law & Order*, I love to watch the courtroom drama unfold. The one who asks the questions is the one who controls the tempo of the courtroom. It is the same in sales. When we ask the questions and then really listen to the answers, we begin to create a relationship with our potential customer. Listening is the greatest skill of any salesperson. People will tell you what they need and want from your product or service, which is the reason they agreed to meet with you in the first place. All you need to do is *ask*. If you do, often what you find is the customer actually will sell themselves on your product or service.

The best sales presentation simply fits the needs of the client to the features and benefits of your product or service. It is really a lesson in matchmaking. You wouldn't set up your sister on a blind date without asking what she is looking for in a significant other. Why would it be any different for matching your product or service with a client's needs? The simplest of questions to ask are as follows:

- What are you looking for in your service?
- How can a product like ours benefit your organization?

- How long is it taking now for your company to do what our service does for you?
- If you had a magic wand and could change three things about your business, what would they be and why?
- What positive changes *will* you see when this challenge is met?
- What do you hate or what frustrates you about your business or process?
- If we were able to grant at least one of your wishes, would you be interested in discussing a business partnership with us?

Many of these questions will get to an emotional and vulnerable level. Vulnerability creates connection. Of course, depending on what you're selling, these questions would be tailored to meet the benefits of your product or service. In the earlier pen example, the easiest way to start out your presentation is: "Thanks for meeting with me to discuss my pen. Do you use pens a lot in your business? What do you like or dislike about the pens you are currently using? How might a new pen help you in your day?" Then sit back and listen. Two ears . . . one mouth.

Really listen. Take notes. Respond by asking for clarification to ensure you have heard him or her and understand what that person needs and wants. Many salespeople, including me, get so excited when we hear that our customer has a need that we can help solve. It is my "superhero" complex that really gets me in trouble! I used to desperately want to show my customers that my product or service was the panacea cure-all that could beam a ray of sunshine on their business and life. So, after hearing their first "magic wand wish," I would jump in and "feature vomit" all over them just because I learned one thing about their business. Not good.

I was fortunate to have been trained by Beverly Steiner. I learned from Beverly every time I was with her, whether one on one or in a large training class at Keller Williams Realty. She taught me that the best salespeople keep asking more questions until *all* of a client's needs and wants are uncovered. Put a star or highlight next to the needs you *know* you can help him or her achieve. Sometimes a person's most important needs are the second, third, or fourth ones mentioned.

As stated earlier, vulnerability creates connection. Your prospective client needs to feel safe to share with you some of their professional vulnerabilities. Active listening and repeating that you understand their needs will allow them to be more vulnerable. It will help them open up to you and share some of the core needs and wants for their business. If we jump in after hearing the first need, whatever connection we created will be broken. Keep asking, and more importantly, keep listening to ensure all their needs and wants have been shared with you. Keep asking these simple questions:

- Why is that important to you?
- How does that impact your day?
- How does it affect your team?
- What happens when that doesn't work?

- Who has to stay late or come in early to do that now?
- Have you monetized how that is impacting your bottom line?
- Does that affect morale?
- Is that keeping you from both your personal and professional goals?

When we ask questions and then truly listen to the wants and needs of our clients, we build long-term relationships. We become their business partner, advisor and guide to success. Do you want to "tell and sell" or "listen and learn?" Two ears and one mouth . . .

NOTES

STOP SELLING WHEN THE CUSTOMER SAYS YES!

My son, Nathan, is great at repeating back to me my own fortune cookie comments. Once, when I was asking for help on a project, I had to sell it a bit to him. After some discussion, he agreed and I kept telling him all the great benefits he would have by helping me. After a few minutes of me continuing on with the benefits, he looked at me and said, "Mom, I said *yes*. Stop selling when the customer says *yes*!"

When we listen to the needs of our clients, the selling becomes more of a conversation dialogue rather than a sales monologue. I have seen many salespeople in my career get tripped up over this tried and true adage. When the customer says yes, you are finished! It doesn't matter how long you spent preparing the most amazing sales presentation. It doesn't matter that you were only on the third of five points you wanted to make. It doesn't matter that you budgeted ninety minutes for this meeting and it has only been twenty. When the customer says *yes* . . . stop selling!

Remember, the meeting is about the customer, not you. During a sales presentation, I often write the acronym, *WAIT* at the top of my notes. The acronym stands for Why Am I Talking? This goes hand in hand with two ears and one mouth. Once we have heard the needs and wants of our client, we can then present solutions. The enthusiasm we have for our solution can be transferred. The potential client learns to understand that your product or service will help him or her close the gap of where that person is and where he or she wants to be. Enthusiasm sells. When the customer is enthusiastic, you have transferred your enthusiasm to them. Usually, this shows up as the customer saying *yes*! Any more words coming out of your mouth will only dilute the energy. Stop talking!

Typically, the customer will say yes in one of two ways.

The first way is after you have built rapport, asked consultative questions, presented appropriate solutions based on the needs of the client, and asked if the customer is ready to get started. When the customer says yes, then get started! Whatever your next step is to move from the sale to implementation, do it! Congratulations, you have done your job well! Get the commitment, the paperwork signed, the implementation date scheduled, or whatever your next step is for your product or service. Great work!

The second way they say yes is in the middle of your presentation. The customer looks to you and says, "What do we need to do to get started?" It can be a bit disarming when the customer closes themselves. Congratulations, you have done your job well! It is okay that you didn't get through every single point of your presentation. Everyone processes information differently. When the customer is ready to go, you need to be ready to go with him or her. Stop talking. Take the next steps and keep taking care of your customer.

Many salespeople get so focused on the process of presenting their product or solution that they fail to pay attention to the buying signals of the client. I have been in the room with salespeople who continue to sell themselves after the client has said, "Great! What is the next step?" Salespeople get paid when they close transactions, not for how long their sales presentation is or if they covered every item in their presentation. Part of being a great salesperson is to engage with the client. Stop selling when the customer says yes and you too will be a great salesperson.

NOTES

YOU ALWAYS FIND WHAT YOU ARE LOOKING FOR

Ask and it will be given to you; seek and you will find; knock and the door will be opened to you. For everyone who asks receives; the one who seeks finds; and to the one who knocks, the door will be opened (Matthew 7:7-8 NIV).[1]

Although this passage is about prayer, I find this wisdom holds true in many aspects of life, both personally and professionally. A note hangs on my refrigerator since my divorce in 2009. The message reads, "Whatever I ask from life, I will get!" Books and movies like *Think and Grow Rich* and *The Secret* remind us that our words and intentions have power. Tony Robbins, Dale Carnegie, Oprah, and countless others remind us to dream big and keep our eyes open for opportunity. What we look for often shows up for us, usually when we least expect it. However, be aware that this works for both the positive as well as the negative. If you are looking for trouble, you just might find it.

Sam Walton, founder of Walmart, was known for stopping to pick up change on the ground. He was a multi-billionaire who drove an old truck to a small office in a small Arkansas town. People would tease him about stopping to pick up change. I always thought it was a model for finding money and opportunity in unlikely places. While working as a summer college intern for Walmart Stores, Inc. in Bentonville, Arkansas, a few months after Sam Walton passed away, I had the blessing of meeting and having a lengthy conversation with his wife, Helen. She was a remarkable woman who received a Finance degree from University of Oklahoma in 1941 when most women didn't go to college. Mrs. Walton had a keen eye for opportunity as well and guided the company to its success. When I see money on the ground, in Sam Walton's memory, I always reach down and pick it up. I tell my kids, "See, money falls from the sky, easily and freely. All you have to do is pick it up and put it in your pocket."

If you are looking for money on the ground, you will find it. If you are looking for the next great opportunity, you will find it. If you are looking for a great friend, partner, client, or investment, you will find it. The clearer you are on *what* you are looking for, the easier it will be to find it. If you think hard enough, you will see examples of this in your own life. The reticular activator in our brain helps us to filter all the stimuli that hits us each day. The best example of this in action is when you are planning to buy a new car. If you are interested in a BMW 3 Series, you will be amazed at how many you see on the road! Our brain helps us filter out the things that are not important. When you tell your brain what to find, it does it. That is why vision boards and written goals are so important. Our mind works with images. If you see pictures of what you desire, then the universe will conspire to help you.

Ask . . . for what you want.

Seek . . . for the opportunity.

Knock . . . and the door will be opened for you.

NOTES

DON'T THINK OF JELLY DONUTS

What is vision? Vision is the experience of seeing something in our mind. A number of years ago, I attended a business planning workshop. The trainer reminded the group that our mind works in pictures.

"Don't think of jelly donuts!" he said.

What happened? Immediately, I thought of a jelly donut!

Often, people set goals relating to what they *don't* want versus what they *do* want. If I ask you to think of healthy food choices, most people think of a table filled with fresh fruits and vegetables, lean meats, and whole grains. That's when the universe conspires to help us. Because our brains think in pictures, we are easily drawn to those healthy choices we see in our mind. If we want our bodies to be healthier, it is better to think of all the wonderful healthy food choices we have, rather than thinking about all the sugary and salty delights that are bad for us that we will need to give up. Think of the positive, being in shape rather than the drudgery of dieting and going to the gym.

Sports psychologists tell athletes to focus on the positive, making the shot rather than missing the shot. If a golfer is over a putt and he starts to think, "I hope I don't miss, I hope I don't miss," the chance of him missing are greater than if he tells himself "I got this." If a basketball coach yells to his player, "Don't miss," it is more likely that he is thinking about missing than making. The point is, when at all possible, use positive words and images.

The same principle applies when we set professional goals. We need to train our mind to have positive thoughts and images. Words, along with images, have power.

A good friend of mine was looking for a new sales leadership opportunity. He had reached out to me because I "know everyone" and might be able to help him. I called an owner of a very successful company to determine if he was looking to add leadership. He was! I love to connect people to people, and people to opportunities. I am so fortunate that much of my job is to make friends and then help my friends create opportunities. Want to be my friend?

When I called my friend back to tell him the good news, he expressed immediate concern about the potential opportunity. He started to tell me everything that he was worried about and all the things he didn't want in his next leadership role. Finally, I stopped him and said, "Do you know what you *do* want?" The sooner you are clear on what you *do* want, the easier it is to determine if an opportunity is a good one. When we focus on what we *don't* want, our brains will be focused on finding the negative. When we focus on what we *do* want, our brain can help filter through to find opportunities, options, and positive solutions.

Business opportunities are a lot like dating. If, before the first date, you are worried about whether the other person likes you, what you are going to serve at the wedding, and the name of your first child, then you are going to have problems. Take one positive step at a time. Take the meeting, go on the first date, focus on what you *do* want and you will find it. Your brain and the universe will conspire to help you. Keep the pictures of success, joy, fun, and endless possibilities in your mind. Make sure the picture in your mind is what you want and go for it. And for God's sake, don't think about jelly donuts!

NOTES

LUCK IS WHEN OPPORTUNITY MEETS PREPAREDNESS

8

LEADERSHIP

In October of 1995, I got married and moved to Honolulu as the wife of a naval officer. After we set up our new home, I needed a job. Previously, I enjoyed a very successful career with Automatic Data Processing (ADP) on the mainland. However, at that time, ADP did not have any offices in Hawaii. The economy wasn't exactly the best, so the only sales job I could find was selling Canon copiers. I knew nothing about copiers. I had the additional disadvantage of barely being able to pronounce the street names on the island. Undeterred, within a few months, I was a top producing copier salesperson.

I achieved this goal by doing the basic task of door knocking. Door knocking or foot canvasing for business was something I had been doing since I was six years old, selling candy bars to raise money for St. Agnes School. I would foot canvas dozens of office doors every day. Most of the time, I was reminded of the "No soliciting" sign on the front door. "What? I'm sorry, I thought that said 'No Smoking!'" was my usual response.

One day, while knocking on the door in an office building, someone asked me if I liked my job. I said, "Well, it's a job." The door happened to be the door of a sales placement company. The gentleman who had asked me that question said, "Wow! You don't see many people out knocking on doors anymore." I lived by the basic sales principle that the more doors I knocked on in a day, the more opportunities I would have for a sale. Immediately, the gentleman got my contact information and said he had an opportunity for me. The next thing I knew, I had a few interviews over the phone for a position as a pharmaceutical sales rep for Abbot Laboratories. They liked me enough on the phone to fly me to Irvine to meet the sales leadership team face to face. Now I had to use my real sales skills to get the job.

The first time I heard the phrase "Luck is when opportunity meets preparedness," I was about to meet the regional manager of Abbot Laboratories. It was down to one other candidate and me for the job. This was 1996, and the Hawaii job market was terrible at best. This was a huge opportunity for me. I actually don't even remember the name of the woman I met with that day. I do remember being partly intimidated (I don't easily intimidate), as well as inspired. She had an energy and presence that exuded success and confidence. I shared the story I just shared above with her.

"I guess I was just lucky to have knocked on that door," I said as humbly as possible.

"Luck is when opportunity meets preparedness," she said.

She was right. And yes, I got the job! To this day, it still seems the harder I work, the luckier I get. So, be prepared, work hard, seek opportunities, and see how lucky you can truly be.

NOTES

DOES THE AUDIO MATCH THE VIDEO?

9

LEADERSHIP

My mom used to bust me because I was sneaky. She *hated* sneakiness and was very vocal about that. In my youth, I was pretty good at telling half-truths. I am not a very good liar, but I was good at lying by omission. Do your actions match up with who you say you are? When other people see you—co-workers, teammates, your family, your children—do they see your actions in direct alignment with what you say is important to you?

As I mentioned previously, I am a big fan of the old TV show *Law & Order*. I will watch hours of reruns. Every once in a while, the transmission will be out of sync. The actor's lips move just about a second behind the sound. It is odd to watch the actor's lips not quite match up to what they are saying. This goes for those who are around us when we are acting out of alignment with our values, saying one thing and doing another. Even though *Law & Order* is just a TV show, it is a great study of human behavior. The detectives often solve the crime because the suspect's words and actions are out of sync.

Our actions demonstrate our commitment. Always. Where you spend your time and energy daily is where you are most committed. Obviously, there are parts of our jobs that aren't the most fun, yet are still very important. When we are committed to the results of those actions, then the commitment level to the task increases. If we say we are committed to good health but proceed to have donuts every day, drink lots of sugary beverages, and never exercise, are we really committed? If I am committed to meeting my sales goals for the quarter and do no lead generation, am I really committed to my own success? Sometimes the role of the sales leadership team is to help salespeople get out of their own way and be accountable to their commitments.

When I would sit down with a coaching client who was telling me one thing and doing another, we would have a grownup conversation about commitment. As soon as the focus was shifted from the activity to the outcome, their commitment to the activities increased. It's okay to like some parts of lead generation better than others. It is okay to have fear about it. When the commitment to the result is clear, the fear diminishes. Courage is not the absence of fear; it is the knowledge that something else is more important.

Chuck coaches high school basketball. He often asks his players if they want to win. Of course, they say yes. He then goes on to tell them that if they truly want to win, they must want to do everything it takes to win: lift weights, run sprints, shoot thousands of shots, eat well, hydrate, and get plenty of rest.

The same goes for business. If you want to be successful, you need to want to do every task and activity that will take you to that success: making calls, meeting new clients, marketing yourself, taking classes, and holding yourself accountable. You need to have a "want to" mentality versus the "have to" mentality. See if you can adjust your attitude from grumpily *having to* do something, to happily *wanting to* do something. I guarantee you will create a more successful you and be more pleasant to those around you. It isn't enough to say you want something. Your actions must demonstrate that want. So make sure your audio matches your video.

NOTES

WHAT DO YOU WANT? (10)

I confess . . . I was a Catholic school girl. I attended St. Agnes, and later St. Francis, for elementary school. And I advanced to Carondelet High School, though I must admit I spent a large majority of my time at De La Salle, the boys' school across the street. I then received a degree in marketing from Santa Clara University. All this Catholic education means I started selling, aka fundraising, at a very early age. Luckily for me, it came naturally.

My first exposure to foot canvasing, or door knocking, took place in first grade. We were tasked with selling boxes of peanut butter and chocolate candy bars. The student in each class who sold the most boxes would win a trip to the amusement park, Great America. I thought that sounded like a great day for a six year old! I figured if I sold five boxes of candy, with twenty bars in each box, I would win the contest. I took my plan to my mom. The plan was to wear my St. Agnes uniform as I went around selling the candy bars to the neighbors. My dad would walk with me and I would do the talking. I sold the first box in an hour. When the contest ended, I was on my way to Great America. That was my first taste of what it meant to be a top producer! From that moment on, I wanted nothing less.

I continued to be the top fundraiser for my class every year, even when I moved schools and fundraising went from candy to "wheel-a-thons." A *wheel-a-thon* is like a walk-a-thon except with bikes, where you are sponsored for each lap you complete. Although, in seventh-grade, I got beat out by a first-grader whose only sponsor was his very wealthy parents. I was so mad! My parents had taught me to go out and earn my own success. It frustrated me that I had done all that hard work only to get beat out by a kid whose parents had "bought" him the prize. So my eighth-grade year, I decided I wasn't going to be bitter, I was going to be better!

I was additionally motivated that year because my father had forbidden me from buying a very popular boom box that was so prevalent in the mid-1980s. My dad believed that the size of a boom box was inversely proportional to the size of the person's brain. As fate would have it, the prize for winning the top fundraising award for the *wheel-a-thon* that year was a boom box! I was so focused on my goal that I didn't care if someone's parents wanted to contribute extra money. I was going to WIN! I knocked on hundreds of doors, spent hours after school every day asking for donations, and was committed to getting that boom box. I was committed to my goal and was willing to do whatever it took to achieve it (see chapter 9).

After the final numbers were tallied at the school assembly, the winners were announced. Each class had a top fundraiser and then there was the overall winner. I could see the boom box for the top fundraiser and I prayed I had won it. When my name was announced as the top fundraiser for the school, the president of the parent council handed me the prize. The president that year happened to be my dad, Gene Dallosto. The smile on my mother's face was priceless. She knew how much my dad hated boom boxes. Despite his dislike for the prize, he proudly handed it over to his daughter who had worked so hard to earn something she wanted so badly. My parents' pride, as well as the pride I had in my own accomplishment, was the true grand prize!

I have dozens of stories like that one. I once sold 106 pizzas my freshman year of high school for a fundraiser. The runner up sold twenty-eight. In my first corporate sales job after college, I earned the President's Club award in only ten months. The President's Club is an awards trip for the top sales people in the company. I managed to keep my real estate office profitable during the credit crisis of 2008. I lost thirty-five pounds in 2012 to achieve my health goal and to be a good healthy role model for my kids. I don't mention these things to brag. I mention them as demonstrations of what can be accomplished when you truly focus on your goals, and then do everything you can to commit to achieving them.

I have often remarked, "I will do almost anything for a $10 gift card!" Yes, there are often financial benefits that come with achieving these goals. Many times, though, I was just satisfied with the recognition. Whether it was a trip, seeing my name at the top of a sales board, or just the personal satisfaction of a job well done, my focus on what I wanted to achieve was always front and center.

As both a real estate coach and sales manager, I have had real estate agents and loan officers come to me for business planning advice. Some have shared very lofty goals, while others are somewhat modest. What do *you* want? If you want it, we can make a plan to get you there. However, you need to want more than just the results. Wanting it includes wanting to do all the activities and commitments that get you there. It is about wanting to take the journey that gets you to your destination. So ask yourself: What do I want? If you want it badly enough, you will commit to do whatever it takes to get there.

DON'T GET BITTER, GET BETTER!

When my very competitive son, Nathan, was ten years old, he was playing basketball for his Catholic Youth Organization team. His dad was the coach. The game was close and tensions were running high. Nathan was hit in the face by an opposing player, but no foul was called. He was bleeding a little from his mouth, so his oldest sister, Kelsey, and I took him to the bathroom to clean up his face. Nathan was crying and visibly upset.

Once we got him cleaned up and the bleeding had stopped, he was able to say through his tears.

"Mom, the other team isn't playing fair! They are cheating! The referees don't see it!"

He was clearly frustrated and bothered.

Kelsey is the kindhearted and compassionate soul in our family. She hugged him. I am not as kind as Kelsey.

I took a different approach. Remembering my seventh-grade *wheel-a-thon* defeat, I repeated to him what I had told myself. I said:

"Don't get bitter, get better! Don't you ever complain that you are losing because someone isn't playing fair or because of the officials. You go out there and be so good that it doesn't matter what the other guy is doing. It doesn't matter what the officials see or don't see. You get so much better at what you do that it doesn't matter what anyone else does!"

Kelsey looked at me like I was the worst mother *ever*! Nathan's first look was shock, then it settled in for him. He went back into the game and led the team in scoring for the remainder of the game. During one of the timeouts, he looked back at me and said, "Mom, I got better!" and smiled. The team won the game. At that time, I don't think I even realized the strength of the lesson. As Nathan and his sisters continued to play sports, they learned to focus on what they could do and not focus so much on what their competition was doing.

Chuck, who coaches high school basketball, tells his players, "You can control two things: effort and attitude." Attitude helps us with perspective, mindset, visualization, and sportsmanlike conduct. A bad attitude is like a flat tire: until you change it, you are not going anywhere.

As a sports fan, I have seen people who have great talent with terrible attitudes. The player who complains anytime things don't go his or her way. The player who continually blames the other guy—his opponent, officials, fans, media, etc. I have also seen players like Derek Jeter and Jackie Robinson who have great talent and even better attitudes. They won and lost gracefully. Embrace all the things that don't go your way, and learn from them to be better next time.

There are thousands of books, videos, and movies about attitude. Pick your favorite quote about attitude and read it daily. Be committed each day to getting better. Give your best effort and have a great attitude. The next time things don't go quite right for you, commit to being better not bitter.

NOTES

LIFE DOESN'T HAPPEN TO YOU

Throughout most of my life, and especially as a young adult, I have often been told I was too loud, too aggressive, too impatient, too ambitious, too focused on success, too passionate, too inquisitive, too curious, too pushy, too sports oriented, too flirtatious, too bossy, too . . . fill in the blank. I spent most of my young adult life apologizing for who I am.

It seemed the only place that I felt these "too" qualities were beneficial was when I was in a sales role. As a professional salesperson, these sorts of qualities are often encouraged. Though as a *saleswoman*, I occasionally ran into trouble. It was OK to surpass my quota and exceed my goals, it wasn't okay to be "one of the boys."

When I was engaged to be married at twenty-three, I decided that my cousin, Andrea, was going to be my role model. She had a wonderful marriage, three fantastic boys, a part-time job that she had for twenty-plus years, a wonderful home, family dinners, and the typical small town sort of life. Years later, after my divorce, I told my teenagers about picking Andrea as my role model. They laughed and looked at me like I had three heads!

"Why?" they asked. "You are *nothing* like Andrea!"

Hence, the divorce. The person I thought I was "supposed to be" was very different than who I actually am. Unfortunately, it took some dramatic life changes and a lot of personal introspection for me to realize that.

Divorce is hard on everyone. This is not therapy, just an opportunity to use my experience to make a point. We all have moments in our lives when it feels like something "happened" to us. It didn't. Instead, we did or did not do something that caused the result we are facing today.

I will admit there are times when things do happen that are beyond our control: acts of God, natural disasters, the negligent or criminal acts of another. However, for the most part, we are responsible for our actions and must be accountable for the consequences of those actions.

One of my kids once said, "The B+ vs. the A- happened to me." But in reality, the B+ was the result of my child's efforts, focus, and commitment to the outcome.

When things happen that are obviously out of our control, success becomes a question of our attitude and behavior in responding to what happened. In my experience, when negative things happen to you they are as much a result of your own decisions and actions as when positive things happen to you.

When positive things happen, is it luck or good fortune? No! It was your effort, energy, commitment, and focus to a result. Take ownership of that, too. When your life and/or business is not going in the direction you like, acknowledge it and make something happen to change it.

Zig Ziglar is quoted as saying, "What comes out of your mouth is determined by what goes into your mind."[1]

Your mind is a very powerful search engine. Whatever you put into the search bar, the results will appear. Everyone has experienced putting the "wrong" words into a search and then frantically hitting the back button! When we search for positive thoughts, images, support, and motivation, our brain finds it. If we look for things that are negative or things that *happen* to us, then the Google brain finds that, too!

The sooner you take responsibility for your thoughts and actions and begin holding yourself accountable for what you put into the search of your brain, the better. Soon, you will move from life "happening to you" to "making things happen!"

NOTES

VULNERABILITY CREATES CONNECTION

Brené Brown has a wonderful video called "The Power of Vulnerability" that you can find on the TED Talk website.[1] She made the video as a project and figured only her mother would end up watching it. Millions of views, a book, and support from Oprah proved otherwise. I first watched it at the urging of my college friend, Bill, who felt it would help me deal with some personal challenges. I have not only watched the video dozens of times but shared it both personally and professionally with almost anyone who would listen.

The power of vulnerability is overwhelming. It is why as a Catholic I go to confession. Confession provides me with time for me to be vulnerable before my God as I recite my sins and ask for forgiveness. It is a very powerful experience. The more vulnerable and open I am, the more I can receive the blessings and forgiveness of God.

The same holds true with both my personal and professional relationships. My closest friends are those who were with me during my best and worst times. In both instances, I was open, honest, and transparent with them. I trusted those frew and they were more than trustworthy. Based on that vulnerability, we created a connection that has lasted for decades.

Vulnerability is not easy. It takes courage to open your heart. We face the uncertainty of what the other person might say or think. In my experience, vulnerability is almost always met with acceptance, grace and love. Being vulnerable means a willingness to show we are human. We are all connected at our deepest level with the human experience.

In business, the same vulnerability happens. The best sales presentations are the ones in which the client tells me his or her challenges or failures. One of my favorite questions to a potential client is, "If you had a magic wand and could change three things about your business, what would they be?" It's amazing to see the childlike wonder in a grownup's face as he or she ponders the power of a magic wand. Their answers usually demonstrate a level of vulnerability. They share struggles about their business, but aren't sure how to overcome them. At some level, they are looking for acceptance, grace, understanding, and a glimmer of hope to resolve these issues. When we are vulnerable with each other, we can create both personal and professional connections. Isn't that the purpose of life?

Pat Lencioni, in his book, *The Five Dysfunctions of a Team*, discusses how "vulnerability-based trust" is invaluable to a successful executive team.[2] I believe that to be the case for any team. Learning someone's story can be a simple opportunity for someone to be vulnerable. Where did you grow up as a child? Do you have any siblings? Was there anything unique or challenging about your childhood? Those questions answered within a small team can quickly create vulnerability-based trust.

Lencioni also believes in behavioral assessments, like DISC or Myers-Briggs. These assessments help people understand that some behaviors are just how someone is hardwired vs. an act of defiance or disrespect. Mending relationships and building vulnerability-based trust is much easier when we understand each other's blind spots. "You can't see the forest for the trees" is valuable for our own behaviors. We tend to judge ourselves by our intentions and others by their behaviors. How do you see yourself? How do you see others? Creating vulnerability-based trust opens the door to better communication and understanding in all relationships.

NOTES

THE DISC PROFILE

This chapter isn't about a fortune cookie one-liner at all. Therefore, I apologize and give you permission to skip it if you want. I'm adding it because I mentioned behavioral assessments in the previous chapter and believe they are important in building relationships—which is really what we do in sales. Behavioral assessments can assist leaders in understanding their teams and help salespeople to understand their clients.

When I was eighteen years old, I took the Myers-Briggs personality profiling test. I remember seeing that my "E" for Extrovert was off the charts! I remember also seeing that my "J" for Judging was also very high. It seemed my profile was fairly unique. Even at eighteen, I looked at the synopsis of the profile as a reminder of all the things that I was "too much" of in my daily life. I now realize it was just a validation of me being perfect in my imperfection.

The DISC profile is a non-judgmental tool used for discussion and determination of people's behavioral differences in four major categories: Drive, Influence, Systematic, and Compliance (DISC). This system is used by corporations throughout the United States. I was first exposed to it while interviewing with Keller Williams Realty. I was interviewing for the role in a leadership position where I would have the opportunity to teach and train real estate agents. I took the assessment and reviewed my DISC results with Keith Robinson, who would become my new boss and friend. We reviewed the DISC profile and immediately Keith mentioned that our profiles were very similar.

As we went through the assessment, it was a bit eerie how accurately it described me. I began apologizing for being impatient, too social, too goal-oriented, and for my poor attention to detail. All of my life I had been apologizing for being too ambitious and felt it would be a good idea to get ahead of it early with a potential employer.

Keith stopped me. "You actually have the exact personality profile of a Fortune 500 CEO. Your profile is a perfect match for a leadership role here." He encouraged me to just be me.

It was one of the most liberating conversations of my life. I learned that my profile had its benefits and drawbacks and how to adjust my natural style as needed. The greatest lesson I received from the DISC personality profiling system was acceptance. Acceptance of how God made me. Acceptance of how God made others who were different, not better or worse, greatly helped me with communication. It gave me the opportunity to own my stuff and have a new perspective on others.

In short, DISC is a simple and easy to understand profiling system that greatly improves communication and understanding.

D profiles are task- and goal-focused. D's are all about the speed and volume of accomplishing tasks. The mantra for a "D" is "I can do it!"

I profiles are characterized by being "people focused." "I's often use the word "who" when looking for solutions. They are generally the life of the party. They pride themselves on having never met a stranger, ever.

S behavioral profiles make up a large percentage of the US population. An S profile places a high value on systems. They, too, are people focused and are great team members. "Slow and steady wins the race" is a common phrase for the High "S" profile.

C profiles are task- and precision-focused. Thank goodness! High C profiles tend to be people who write code for programs, build bridges and buildings, and do our taxes. The mantra for a High C is "It doesn't matter how long it takes, as long as it is done right!"

Our behaviors are made up of some combination of each of these. Though what makes us different is the level of each. Each person usually has a high profile in one or two of these. However, in any situation, everyone can utilize the behaviors of each of these profiles. There is no wrong or right personality profile. Each profile, or combination thereof, is what makes us who we are.

The best analogy I can use for understanding the DISC profile is to think about doctors. If you think about the variety of doctors out there and how it relates to DISC, it may help you understand how the profiles match.

- High D—Emergency Room Doctor: speed and task. Stop the bleeding! Triage and get ready to send to the specialist or next appropriate step. The ends justify the means.
- High I—Pediatrician: speed and people. Pediatricians can connect with all members of the family and are highly empathetic. They can communicate and interact with a five-year old who does not want his or her shots and also with the worried parent.
- High S—General Surgeon: slow and steady with the team. They do the same surgeries and procedures every day and have done so for years. They work well with the surgical staff and colleagues at the hospital, and have a steady process for how they do every surgery.
- High C—Brain Surgeon: get it right! Process and accuracy. I want my brain surgeon to take as much time as he or she needs to get it right. Speed is not important, accuracy is.

There are several companies that do DISC profiling. If you would like more information or to have a DISC profiling assessment for your team, please visit www. CapisceConsulting.com. Today, I have a much better understanding of myself and others because of my education on the DISC profiling system. Because of that, I am able to work with and communicate with my co-workers and clients. Once you understand, you can begin to learn and grow.

NOTES

DON'T FORCE IT

This chapter is dedicated to my dad, Gene. My dad and sister, Karolyn, are both math majors. I'm pretty sure they both think I am from a different planet. My dad and I look alike and that is where the similarities end. Since my dad is a High C (as discussed in the DISC chapter), analytics, numbers, procedures and systems all come very naturally to him. He is the guy who actually reads the instructions before putting something together. In fact, I believe he actually reads them twice!

Once, we went fifteen rounds over my philosophy on how to handle a computer issue. My argument was that I should just hit a few buttons and figure it out quickly. He wanted to get out the operations manual before I touched anything. My father is always reminding me, "Don't force it." I first heard the expression when I was a kid as I was either putting something together or taking something apart. Of course, as an impatient person, and a child, I had to test the theory. As I usually found out, father knows best.

My efforts to do it my way and force it often resulted in less than a desirable result.

"Don't force it" can be applied to sales as well. The best opportunities, clients, promotions, etc., are often the ones that seem to present themselves seamlessly. We have all had experiences with clients or prospects in which it felt like wedging a square peg into a round hole. It just doesn't work.

These experiences drain our energy, rob us of our joy, and make us question our instincts. The "don't force it" philosophy is closely analogous to the "trust your gut" philosophy.

When I read Joel Osteen's book, *Your Best Life Now*, one of the messages in the book that I took away is when we work in God's plan, it is effortless. However, when we work outside of God's plan, it is rough and draining.[1]

In sales, we need to trust our internal guidance system. Do you need everyone you meet to be your client? How many clients do you really need to meet or even exceed your goals? It is OK to fire a client. It is better to step away from a bad opportunity or business relationship than to have him or her take time away from your good ones.

Don't force it! Sometimes it is okay to read the directions, take a deep breath, look around, and remember that you are amazing. Your product, service, experience, and talents are not for everyone. They are for the clients who are a joy to serve. They are for those clients who you look forward to working with, even during a tough transaction. Your willingness to be vulnerable, to share your gifts and your wisdom, is what will get you to success. No need to force it.

SALES IS A CONTACT SPORT

Regardless of technology, sales is a belly to belly business. Texting, emailing, websites, apps, and other fantastic technology tools are great. These tools need to be leveraged for the opportunity to get face to face. At the end of the day, your success is predicated on your contacts. Whether you play the numbers game in which X number of contacts, gets you Y number of leads, who turn into Z number of appointments, who turn into closed transactions, or you focus on deliberate and consistent contact with key referral partners and advisors, it is all about *contacts*.

Touch people, not paper. Stay focused on contacts and the results will follow. Use email to generate interest. Use the phone to make an appointment. Use social media for research and connections. Use handwritten notes to stand out from the crowd. All of these need to lead to contacts. People do business with people they like and trust. How can they get to like and trust you via email?

Did you decide to get married over an email, text, or video chat? Was your first date arranged on email or over the phone? You may have used those tools to help create and even deepen the relationship. I imagine that the true connection happened face to face. Creating the moment to sit across from each other is what builds the trust. The energy shared, the vulnerability, the laughter, is what created the connection. Think about your best personal and professional relationships. Are they relationships made only via instant message and email?

Most people want to connect with you. So tell your story. Shake their hand. Share a smile or a laugh. There is no doubt that there are some great technology tools, like videos, blogs, and live chat that can aid in creating connection. However, they need to be leveraged correctly to bring you face to face, belly to belly business opportunities, which are the most successful and long lasting. Remember, sales and life are both contact sports.

TWO WRONGS DON'T MAKE A RIGHT

17

LEADERSHIP

My mother was proudly 100 percent Irish. Nothing would "get her Irish up" more than compounding a bad decision with a worse decision. Two of her favorite phrases were, "If you don't want anyone to know it, don't do it" and "Two wrongs don't make a right." We discussed the former in chapter 3. Even though she passed away in 1998, whenever I hear the latter phrase, I still hear her voice as if it were yesterday.

There is obviously a moral aspect to this teaching. Mom was big on taking responsibility for your actions. It would incense my mother if you did something wrong and then compounded the injury by lying about it! Her number one pet peeve was lying. It was bad enough that you did something wrong. Don't lie about it. It will only make it worse. "Two wrongs don't make a right, Katey!" We are human. We make mistakes. We have to own them.

We have the same responsibility in our business

lives. Negotiations, by their very nature, have an adversarial tone to them. Often, we allow our own behavior to be dictated by the behavior of those on the other side of the negotiation. Ultimately, your job is to represent your client, your company, or your service to the best of your ability.

You know the right thing to do. Do it. It is easy to mirror the behavior of others. Doing the right or healthy thing isn't always the easy thing. In fact, sometimes doing the right thing is downright hard. Creating a win-win for all parties should be the goal. Be the calming force, the solution-oriented voice in the crowd, the one people come to because you'll do the right thing. Take the high road, even if somebody else started it. I am a big believer in "right is right." If you have to think about whether something is right, it probably isn't. Don't let others steer you down the dark side, because often it can be difficult to turn around. Let your integrity, perseverance, and commitment be your guide. If two wrongs don't make a right, I bet the inverse is also true. Two rights don't make a wrong.

CHAMPAGNE EMERGENCY 18

LEADERSHIP

Why does it seem that every time we are going to celebrate something, we don't have the champagne chilled? My dad likes to say that there always needs to be a bottle of champagne chilling in the refrigerator in case of a champagne emergency. What is a champagne emergency? It is an occasion that arises that calls for a celebration. Your friend comes over to tell you she got a promotion, is buying a new house, is engaged, etc. Do you have a bottle of champagne ready to open for these celebrations?

Once, at a sales rally, I had the opportunity to listen to *New York Times* best-selling author and motivational speaker Clint Swindall. Clint and his wife would stock up on champagne for this very reason. Over time, they would buy champagne on sale and have plenty on hand for any celebration. Of course, if you buy champagne every time it is on sale, you end up with lots of champagne. So, Clint and his wife started to look for opportunities to celebrate. B+ on a test . . . open the champagne! It rains after many days of drought . . . open the champagne![1] You get the idea. They looked for reasons to celebrate and found them! As I mentioned in chapter 6, I am a big believer that we always find what we are looking for in our lives.

Do you look for opportunities to celebrate even the smallest victories? It is the same part of your brain, the reticular activator, which causes you to see so many new red cars on the road the day after you purchase one. It is like you have never seen many red cars before and now they are everywhere. How does that happen? We tell our brains, consciously and sub-consciously, what to look for in our environment. When we tell our brains to look for opportunities to celebrate, we find them.

What kinds of opportunities can we celebrate every day? Often, small successes gradually lead to big successes. When I was in outside sales, meeting cli-ents face-to-face, I celebrated on the days I closed a sale. Of course, depending on the type of job I had, sometimes I got to celebrate twice per week, but with large accounts jobs, it might have been only twice a year! If you sell a big-ticket item or only look at the month-end financials to celebrate, those victories can seem few and far between. So look for little reasons to celebrate!

Did you make your follow-up calls today? Did you get in your morning workout today? How many appointments do you have booked for the week? Did you do something that scared you and will move you closer to your goals? If you answered yes to any of these, you have a reason to celebrate!

You don't necessarily need to open a bottle of champagne. Figure out your own reward: a cup of your favorite coffee, a walk around the block, or a massage. I think you get the idea. Celebrate even your smallest victories! Have enough of these small daily victories and soon you will be pouring the champagne to celebrate your very own championship season. So make sure you have that bottle of champagne chilling in the refrigerator. You never know when a champagne emergency might happen!

NOTES

APPLE . . . TREE

Apple . . . tree is a short form of the old adage: The apple doesn't fall far from the tree. It is the quote that binds generations to the craziness and composition that is our family.

My oldest daughter, Kelsey, has my skin tone and my eye and hair color. She also has her mother's and grandmother's curse of crying when she is tired.

My middle child, Erika, looks absolutely nothing like me. In fact, you wouldn't even know she was mine until she opens her mouth. She has my spunk, my lack of filter, and my competitiveness. I know she has what it takes to change the world someday.

My youngest, Nathan looks just like his dad. He has my mother's skin-tone but my personality. Nathan is like his mother in that neither one of us has ever met a stranger. My mom used to say, "Katey would never have been kidnapped; she would have gone willingly." Nathan is the same way. We share a love of baseball and a similar sense of humor.

As for me, I look like my dad but have my mother's personality mixed in with a whole bunch of crazy from my aunts.

You can tell your own similar stories about your family. We are the sum of the total of all our parts. Apple . . . tree is the basic idea that we all are a combination of our genetic makeup and our own experiences. We are a product of nature as well as nurture. Our looks, our idiosyncrasies, and our thinking are molded by our families and our environment. That environment is our families, friends, and co-workers.

The point is, as my older readers will remember from Popeye, "I am what I am." Embrace who you are and the wonderful combination of biology and experiences that formulated you. Continue to take all the gifts that have been given to you, mix them with the blessings we receive every day, and continue to be the best you that you can be.

Now does that mean we have no ability to change? In a business situation, does that mean we remain set in our ways and rigid in our thinking? No! It means we take the set of skills, values, and qualities that we have been blessed with and then use them in the best possible way, adapting them to the issue at hand to achieve the best possible outcome.

To continue to shape who we are, we must continue to surround ourselves with the people, leaders, teachers, books, seminars, and podcasts that will help us develop and grow our own tree. Continue to surround yourself with other trees that help you be the best tree you can be. Make sure you are planted in the right orchard.

Understand that someday, if not already, you will be bearing your own fruit. In your family and in business, you probably already are a tree to someone. Be aware that you have a substantial impact and influence on those around you. Make sure your words and actions are positive. So, the next time you hear "Apple . . . Tree", you know it is a compliment.

NOTES

PRAY FOR THEM

When I was in middle school, I was bullied. I had one of the best grades in class and was teased for it. The fact that I was in my awkward phase didn't help either. A bad haircut, puberty at its finest, and thick glasses compounded the effects. I fully embraced my nerdyness. I was teased about everything. Kids were mean and called me a dog. One time, they even brought dog biscuits to school and gave them to me during lunch. I was miserable.

I was forty before I had the confidence to believe I was beautiful. Even today, I still have my moments of doubt and insecurity. We are all works in progress. Okay, that wasn't the point of the story. The infuriating part was coming home mad after being teased all day at school, only to have my mother, a "Super Catholic" (her words not mine), tell me to pray for them. Mom would remind me that people who tease and make fun of others are doing it out of their own insecurities and that we need to pray for them. Really?

Recently, I was sitting at a restaurant waiting for my friends to join me for dinner. Country music was playing over the speakers. A beautiful song about a recent breakup began to play. The lyrics described this sad young man listening to a sermon in church that stated we should pray for those who have hurt us. The tempo of the music increased and the lyrics quickly changed. The message altered to the young man praying that the brakes go out on the car of the woman that hurt him, a flower pot drop on her head, and none of her dreams come true. I almost spit out my water! I had been lulled into the mantra of my mother's "pray for them" only to be transformed back to my middle-school years wanting bad things to happen to those who hurt my feelings. I totally commiserated with the singer.

The song might encapsulate our moments of hurt and anger. I believe that there are two emotions: love and fear. Fear is where all negative emotions live: doubt, envy, rage, sadness, anger, etc. Love is where all the positive emotion lives: joy, happiness, excitement, etc. Fear is finite. Fear breeds scarcity— the idea that there is only so much to go around, so I better get mine. Love is infinite. There is plenty of love and abundance out there for everyone.

The song that embraces the notion of praying for bad things to happen to someone who has harmed us is obviously tapping into the fear part of our emotions. My mom's version of "pray for them" is a bit more focused on the love side of things. When someone hurts us, or does something out of fear, our first reaction is that of retaliation. "I'll show them!" We lash back out at those who have lashed at us.

Next time, instead of instantly reacting, take the time to formulate a response. Take a deep breath. Maybe say a prayer for them. Understand that they might be living in a place of fear. Make the choice to live in a place of love. Pray that someday they can live in a place of love, instead of fear. For it is in a place of love that we find solutions, joy, and collaboration.

My mother's "pray for them" mantra reminds me that I have a choice. We can choose the path of fear and negativity or the path of love and positivity. I have heard her voice when it comes to business negotiations. When in the midst of a negotiation, is it the fear that is causing you anger? Is the party on the other side fearful, too? What is the fear of the party on the other side of the negotiation? How can being a solution and abundance thinking person help everyone to be happy with the outcome? Are you praying for them to be in a better place or praying that bad things happen to them? Hopefully, you can find the love in your heart to pray for the best in people.

When we can pray, regardless of our religious beliefs, compassion and love always win. So the next time someone does something you don't like, pray for them.

NOTES

TEARS ARE PASSION MANIFESTED

I am a crier. I cry at commercials, auditions on reality TV shows, weddings, funerals, and when I am tired, hungry, or frustrated. It doesn't take much to make me cry. When I fight, I cry. When I am happy and proud, I cry. When I am sad or joyful, I cry. Once, during a disagreement with Chuck, he said, "I love your passion. Your tears are passion manifested." It is along the same lines of Jimmy Valvano's ESPY's speech, "If you laugh, you think and you cry, that's a full day."[1]

What is your passion? Sometimes passion is difficult to discern. Business strategists and leadership coaches can't help you find your passion. They can help you turn your passion into production, but they can't create your passion for you—that's for you to determine. Passion is something that burns deep within each of us. Your passion may only come out in what makes you cry. It might be an injustice. Your tears can motivate you to take action against that injustice. It can be in reading a book about a particular viewpoint or part of the world. If there are moments in a movie that bring you to tears, you are uncovering your passion. What makes you cry?

The tears that stream down your face are the path to your passion. Maybe it is the tears of others. One of my first real estate clients were first time home buyers. They were an adorable young couple looking to buy in 2004. It was a crazy hot market and we were constantly getting outbid and they were discouraged. When we finally got them into a very small, dark, and dated condominium unit, they were elated. I will never forget giving them the keys to their first home and watching the tears stream down their faces. It was at that moment that I realized my passion was helping other people achieve their dreams. That is my passion. Find yours and don't be afraid to reveal it to the world with your tears.

IF YOU ARE NICE TO PEOPLE, YOU GET MORE STUFF

The *Today Show* did a "Rossen Report[1]" to determine if travelers received more benefits when they were nice to people. The results were overwhelming. They concluded that when you are nice to people, you get more stuff. The "nice" travelers received free upgrades, waived fees, and additional perks by simply being nice when asking for things. When we are nice, people respond in turn with other nice gestures.

There is a little of "closed mouths don't get fed" in this concept. A friend of mine told me his grandfather walks into every restaurant, sits down, and says with a smile, "What can I get here for free?" My friend tells me it is amazing what he actually gets!

This is Chuck's mantra everywhere he goes. He greets the staff at stores, restaurants, and hotels like old friends. He shakes their hand, looks them in the eye, and says, "It's great to see you, thanks for being here today!" He may never have been in that town before, but the people always respond as if he is an old friend. It's awesome!

Whenever I go to a restaurant, I always ask my servers their name. Then to remember it, I ask him or her either how they spell it or if there is a story connected to it. During that sixty-second interaction, I often say that person's name out loud five to ten times. By the simple act of learning his or her name, I create a connection. During the course of the meal, if I should need something, I can call him or her by name and I don't have to wave and say, "Excuse me!" It also makes that person feel special. Everyone likes to hear his or her own name. It is amazing the increased level of service we get!

In sales, I always found the best negotiations were with people who were nice and professional. Even though we all have a job to do, we can still be nice. A win-win approach to negotiations is a great start. Respect the other person and his or her role in the negotiation. We all need to go home at the end of the day to our loved ones. When you are kind and ask nicely for things, people are naturally inclined to help you.

See what more stuff you can get today by being nice!

IT'S ALL ABOUT THE FUNDAMENTALS

23

I am a stickler for fundamentals—When my son, Nathan, was playing baseball, I was his coach for the first three years. As soon as he started pitching, I knew I was in over my head. Part of my reason for coaching is my love of baseball. The other part was to instill a commitment to the fundamentals of baseball.

- Run through the first base bag
- Watch your base coaches
- Catch fly balls with both hands
- Run straight ahead, don't look over your shoulder
- Keep your glove in the dirt for ground balls
- Focus on footwork and form at the plate
- Keep your eyes on the ball

All professional baseball players are masters of the fundamentals, well OK, maybe not all. The muscle memory of the fundamentals is what can elevate your game. Smart players know that when your body knows what to do and how to do it, the finesse can come later.

To be truly successful, we all need to master the fundamentals. One way to do this is the 10,000-repetition rule. And, not just 10,000 repetitions but 10,000 "perfect" repetitions. If they aren't perfect, all you are doing is re-enforcing bad habits. Bruce Lee once said, "I fear not the man who has practiced 10,000 kicks once, but I fear the man who has practiced one kick 10,000 times."[1]

Vince Lombardi, the Green Bay Packers Hall of Fame football coach, started every season reminding his players of the fundamentals. I mean the most basic of fundamentals. He would hold up the ball and say, "Gentlemen, this is a football.[2]"

John Wooden, the Hall of Fame basketball coach for UCLA and winner of ten National Championships, would begin the first practice of each new season teaching his players how to put on their socks. If your socks aren't right, your feet aren't right, and that could lead to injury.[3]

These are all great examples of mastering the fundamentals.

Why do we ever leave the fundamentals? What are the fundamentals of sales?

- Marketing consistently: a marketing plan, even a mediocre one, done consistently is better than the best marketing plan done inconsistently or never.
- Lead generation: it is the lifeblood of your business. Whether you lead generate face to face,

over the phone, or door to door, it never stops unless you want your business to stop.

- Client meetings: nothing builds your business faster than creating great relationships with your clients. You can use Skype or video conferencing but nothing beats in-person face to face. People do business with people they like. Todd Duncan shares with his clients and has personally told me, "If you want clients for life, then you have to talk with them during their life."[4]

- Ask! Every sales training program, book, workshop, webinar, etc., all comes down to asking for business. See chapter 1: *Closed Mouths Don't Get Fed*!

- Follow up: the fortune is in the follow-up with your clients. Ask great questions to find their needs, then follow up on those needs.

Fundamentals exist in every aspect of our lives. Fundamentals to good health include making good food choices, drinking plenty of water, exercising, and rest. Fundamentals to romantic relationships include honesty, communication, and creating special moments. I can go on, and so could you. When you focus on the fundamentals, the results will follow. Every time.

NOTES

IF YOU ERASE IT, REPLACE IT!

This is my favorite (time blocking/priority management) tool. I learned about time blocking in 1994 when I started working for ADP. We had four fundamentals of success for the sales team:

- Calling for appointments (6 hours/3 days per week)
- Foot canvassing (6-8 hours/4 days per week)
- Appointments (10 per week)
- Sales meeting and trainings (2 per week)

We were all given a spiral bound calendar book that when laid flat would show each week across the two pages. We were instructed to take four different colored highlighter pens and block out the times for each of our weekly commitments. We were instructed that if we did all of our blocked activities each week, we would meet our weekly quota. Yes, I said "weekly."

Our sales meetings were a form of public humiliation. We had to stand up in front of our peers and leadership each week and say out loud how we did that week against our weekly quota. There was a weekly scoreboard in the main sales room (a.k.a. our shark tank) for all to see. It ranked each salesperson in the company. I think the idea was that the board was a motivator for the true sharks. The non-sharks often would choose another career path.

Because we did our calendar books in pen, we did not erase. If there was a change in something, we simply crossed it out and put it somewhere else on the calendar for that week. It worked for me because I was a top performer and loved the simplicity of the plan and competitive nature of the shark tank.

The model has served me well for over twenty years. In the real estate industry, it seems that most real estate and loan professionals lack training in managing their time and commitments.

When writing down your goals for your business, it ultimately comes down to simple math. Lead generation leads to appointments, appointments lead to clients, clients lead into closed transactions, and the cycle begins again. Focus on *the* weekly activities you *will* need to do to achieve your weekly goals. Put it on your calendar. If it is not in your calendar, it doesn't exist!

When you calendar your most important activities—sales activities, kids' soccer games, date night, and spiritual time—it demonstrates your commitment to each activity. Many people have said that time blocking becomes too restrictive. I find the opposite to be true. If I know the exact number of calls and appointments I need to make in a week to achieve my goals, and I can get those completed sooner, I can take the rest of the week off to go play!

If you need to move a commitment on your calendar, go for it! However, if you do, then you must replace it somewhere else on your calendar for that same week. If you erase it, replace it! The flexibly of your calendar is there. You get to decide your commitments and goals. When you know what you need to accomplish, commit to it weekly.

NOTES

TIME BLOCKING IS YOUR FRIEND

In 1994, I took my first outside sales job with the payroll company ADP (Automatic Data Processing). I was introduced to ADP by one of my mom's teaching students who had a brother that worked there. As luck would have it, my mom, her student, and the student's brother were all Santa Clara University alumni. As I explain in chapter 29, it's not always what you know but who you know.

The connection at ADP was Greg Stivers. Even though he was just twenty-seven years old, his results in outside sales made him a rock star in the world of ADP. In my young mind, he was a legend. He soon became my mentor, my boss, and my friend.

I am not a fan of "reinventing the wheel." If something is working, then I say, "Just copy it until you are ready to make it your own." This led me to ask Greg about his success. He was a huge fan of the sales training and tools that ADP provided. Greg is the one that introduced me to the importance of *time blocking*. The theory is to create your plan on your calendar, then implement your plan.

However, in 1994, time blocking for me amounted to taking a spiral bound annual calendar and laying it out flat on my desk. Each week was spread out nicely over two 8.5" x 11" pages. I was given four colored highlighters. Each color represented an important sales task. The four tasks were: making calls, knocking on doors (foot canvassing), face to face appointments, and office trainings/meetings.

My goals were clear. They were based on simple math: If I lead generated, made my calls and knocked on enough doors, I would get appointments. If I got appointments, I knew I could make a sale. If I made enough sales, I would make my goals.

I went to work time blocking on my calendar for the year. It was then easy to know what I was going to do every day, because it was right there on my daily calendar. As I scheduled appointments with clients, I would place their names in the allotted highlighted slots. I confidently knew if I filled in the blanks for those ten appointment slots each week, I would achieve my goals.

It was amazing how easy and efficient time blocking was. When I had achieved my appointment goal for the day or week, I could then decide if I wanted to push for surpassing my goal or take some down time. By time blocking, I was also able to block out my personal appointments so I would continue to develop my health goals, stay connected with friends and family, and enjoy life on the beach. Time blocking became my friend.

By the time I entered the real estate industry, I had three kids. Time blocking became even more important. Debi Krichbaum, a real estate friend of mine from San Diego and a huge time blocking proponent, reminded me that everything on your calendar is an appointment. No one has to know that the appointment is with your family, friends, or even yourself. Picking up your kids from school is an appointment. Attending your daughter's soccer game is an appointment. Decide what is most important to you. Schedule those appointments first. Then fill in the rest in descending priority.

Debi ended up buying a boat. She was smart enough to name her boat "An Appointment." When people ask, "Where are you, Debi?" She can honestly say, "I'm on An Appointment." I love it!

Time blocking can be your friend. It can also keep you accountable to your goals because they are right in front of you. You can have your own priorities. Here is an example of how you can time block your calendar:

- Time off
  - o vacation time
  - o time you go home and "turn off" work (maybe even change your voicemail)
- Personal commitments
  - o family time
  - o date nights
  - o spiritual wellness
  - o health and fitness

- Lead generation
  - o phone
  - o face to face
  - o marketing
- Appointments
  - o how many appointments a week do you need to meet your goals?
  - o what is your conversion rate?
    (Your conversion rate is the percentage of appointments you need to get an actual client paying for your services.)

There are no real hard and fast rules when it comes to time blocking, but I like these axioms:

- If you erase it . . . replace it!
- If it's not on your calendar, it doesn't exist!

When you make the commitment to time blocking, life gets a little easier. You no longer have that Monday conversation with yourself of "what do I have to get done this week?" It's all set out for you in your calendar. You get to eat the elephant one bite at a time. You can celebrate daily and weekly goals that you set out for yourself that don't necessarily include a closed sale. These little daily victories may lead to a "champagne emergency!"

If you trust the process of time blocking, I promise you the results will follow. So go ahead and meet your new friend—its name is Time Blocking.

COMPLIMENTS ARE GIFTS

Kid birthday parties are always a bit like walking on a land mine. Do you, or do you not, have the kids open the presents in front of all of their five-year-old buddies? What if my child says something ungrateful? What if there are two of the same present? How will my child respond? How will the other kids respond? Or worse, how will the other parents respond?

One year, I decided to take matters into my own hands with my son's fifth birthday party. All the kids wanted Nathan to open his presents so they could play with whatever new toys he received. I had all the kids gather around Nathan so we could practice what to say. "OK kids, every time Nathan opens a present, what do we say?"

"We say, 'oooooh . . . aaaaahhh!' with delight!"

"What if he gets dirty socks for a present?" I asked.

"We say, 'oooooh . . . aaaahhhh.'"

It worked well because every kids' gift received the appropriate amount of "ooooooohs and aaaaahhs" and felt like his or her gift was appreciated.

Why don't we, as adults, do the same thing with compliments? It drives me crazy when I tell someone that her dress is pretty, I like her new haircut, she looks beautiful, or "great work on your presentation" and I get a backhanded negative response.

"Oh, this dress has a stain on it."

"My hair is such a pain to get right."

"I've hardly put on any make-up today."

"My presentation had a lot of mistakes because I was so nervous!"

Even if you don't feel worthy or agree that your dress is pretty, say thank you! Someone just stopped to be vulnerable with you. They have shared something personal about how they feel about you. You respond as if they have just given you dirty socks. If a five-year old can say thank you when grandma gives him or her new underwear for Christmas (like my grandmother did), then you, as a full-grown adult, can say thank you to a compliment.

If you don't drink coffee and I give you a Starbucks gift card, what would you say? I would hope you would say, "Thank you!" But Heaven forbid I pay you a personal compliment, a gift from my heart, and you blow it off. That is rude. Please people, when someone gives you the gift of a compliment, just say thank you. Ok…rant over!

COURAGE IS NOT THE ABSENCE OF FEAR

27

LEADERSHIP

The best part about failure is that the more often you do it, the less fearful you become of it. There is a difference between fear and danger. The danger reflex is good and healthy. It keeps you and your loved ones safe from harm. The fear of doing something that is not dangerous is what holds us back from our truest and best selves.

When my teenagers are afraid of going up to meet another teenager, but then they do it, I have been known to say, "Did anyone burst into flames?" (sarcastically, of course). The comment is designed to remind them that no one died and there is no true danger in doing something that seems scary. It is through the power of doing a fearful thing that courage is built.

Having been in sales my entire life, I know rejection can be scary. There is always the fear that a prospective client will say no. But I push through it because some will say yes.

What is more important to you than the fear of rejection? Is there a goal you want to achieve? Is it the pride of work? Do you want to go on a really great vacation, buy a house, or invest in your future? Those things that are important to you and your family are what will ultimately give you courage to act in spite of your fear.

Without fear, there is no courage. You will enjoy an immense sense of satisfaction once you have the courage to do that which is scary. Your perspective of fear will change once you have had success in merely taking the action toward that goal, regardless of the outcome. Remind yourself of what is really more important.

When I was in sales at ADP, making President's Club was a really big deal. When I was hired at the company, I was told that it would be three years before I could expect to go to President's Club. That was the average. I was given the worst territory in the area and was told that no one who had ever had that territory had ever been to President's Club.

If you know me, telling me what I couldn't do is a good motivator. So, on the rearview mirror of my car, I stuck a Post-it note that read "Bermuda." That was the President's Club destination my first year. Every time I had a fear of canvassing a new area, making a follow-up call, or meeting with an unhappy client, I looked at the Bermuda note. It reminded me that there was something more important than my fear. That year, I made President's Club in ten months and never looked back!

Figure out what is most important to you. Decide what inspires you. We all have that place we want to go or that thing we want to do. Focus on the special people or causes in your life that will give you the courage to overcome your fears. It's OK to have fear; it's even better to be courageous.

NOTES

HOW CAN YOU TEACH A FISH TO CLIMB A TREE?

Once I saw a cartoon. In it the teacher is looking at his students. His students are a monkey, a penguin, an elephant, a fish, a seal, and a dog. The teacher says, "For a fair selection, everybody has to take the same exams: please climb that tree." The large tree in the background is foreboding to the students who will have a challenge climbing it. This cartoon exemplifies the disparity of learning styles amongst allof us. My mother was a teacher of teachers and we often had discussions regarding learning styles. Mom was convinced that my dad was an undiagnosed dyslexic. When we looked at his school report cards, he had poor grades in all of his classes except math, where he scored all A's. Obviously, he was a bright kid who struggled with reading. My dad started programming computers in the late 1960s. He is clearly very bright. Unfortunately, he was being graded on tasks that were not in his natural ability. Using the illustration, he was a penguin being asked to climb a tree.

My second daughter, Erika, has always struggled with reading. At first, I took it lightly.

"She is pretty, blonde, and has beautiful blue eyes. How important is reading?" I said sarcastically to her teacher.

I'm sure that comment took me off the "Mother of the Year" list.

Soon, she was a year or two behind in reading levels. Despite our best efforts to help her, she found reading very difficult. Erika's strength is in her creativity, quick wit, and basic analytic reasoning. She is extremely bright and teachers would remark on her ability to figure out a book's ending by just understanding some basics points early in the story.

Erika was eventually diagnosed with dyslexia, the disorder involving a difficulty in learning to read or interpret words, letters, and symbols. Some notable dyslexics include Richard Branson, Steven Spielberg, Barbara Corcoran, Cher, and Albert Einstein. Once she understood and accepted that she was "different" and not "dumb," she was able to improve her reading. It wasn't easy. It took a lot of hard work on her part and the support of all those around her. In many ways, she was the fish being asked to climb the tree.

We are all blessed with many gifts, just not always the same gifts. That's what makes us great as a society. For Erika, she excels on the soccer field as a goalie and center defender because she is a strong natural leader. She actually sees the field differently than people who are not dyslexic. The greatest gift Erika has given to me is the reminder that we all learn, think, and view things differently. Different is not better or worse; it is just different. It's all about perspective and acceptance.

I know my mother would have been a fierce advocate for Erika. She might have even helped me engage earlier in helping Erika. It is one of many things I wish I could talk to her about with regard to my children.

We are not all monkeys. We are elephants, penguins, dogs, and cats. So it is unfair to judge us on our ability to climb a tree. Intelligence, leadership, skill, and integrity are things that can be measured in multiple ways. We need different perspectives and points of view to achieve our goals. When you are working with your team and/or your clients, remember to include a variety of measurements for discovering needs, goals, and success. Don't ask a fish to climb a tree.

NOTES

AGREE TO DISAGREE

In the eighth grade, I was invited to a party. I was socially awkward and the invite alone was a big deal for me. My mom and I discussed who was going to be there, what sort of party this was going to be, and whether parents would be in attendance. The latter point was a pivotal one. She did not approve of my attending a party without parental supervision. Of course, I was doing my best sales job, saying I was a good girl and would make good choices. She heard my point of view and after some additional discussion, she said, "I agree with your points and we are just going to have to agree to disagree." I did not attend the party.

Even though I didn't get to go to the party, I felt heard and validated. I didn't know it at the time, but it was an invaluable lesson that I use in almost every aspect of my life. I have used that philosophy when discussing religion, politics, and sports. As a parent, I still use mom's words to my own children. Discussions often end with "let's just agree to disagree."

My stepdaughter, Samantha, probably hears it the most. Samantha is one of the most well-read and knowledgeable people I know, especially when it comes to Latin American studies. She is constantly challenging my thoughts and perceptions on third-world countries. Samantha is also a vegetarian. She is a Model UN ambassador (Model United Nations, also known as Model UN or MUN, is an educational simulation and/or academic competition in which students can learn about diplomacy, international relations, and the United Nations). Samantha uses her amazing verbal talents to propel her team to success. Her passion for her causes is unmatched and always a great source of discussion. Often we must "agree to disagree." My hope is that she feels validated and heard. In fact, she often does change my mind and expand my horizons.

Agreeing to disagree is about respect. I don't want or need to change someone else's mind, nor do I want or need my mind to be changed. Respect is a willingness by both parties to hear the other's point of view. In Pat Lencioni's book, *The Five Dysfunctions of a Team*, conflict is a central part of a healthy team.[1]

Music without conflict is dull. Relationships, in which everyone agrees, don't have depth. Differing opinions and points of view are what make companies successful and negotiations respectful. In most organizations, the ultimate decision is that of the leader. The leader must be open to differing points of view to minimize blind spots when making decisions.

No one wants to be thought a "*yes* man." Be willing not only to express your thoughts, but then be willing to listen to others. It is through our varying points of view and perspective that growth truly happens. We don't necessarily need to change each other's minds. We simply need the respect to listen to the other person. By doing so, we validate one another and ultimately help each other to achieve our goals.

NOTES

IT'S NOT ALWAYS WHAT YOU KNOW, BUT WHO YOU KNOW

When I was a senior in high school, I had my heart set on attending Santa Clara University (SCU) after I graduated. Both my mom and grandfather were SCU alumni and I wanted to continue the tradition. My grades were very good, but I had only taken two years of Spanish and they preferred three. The SCU admissions director at the time was Dan Sarancino, who my mother knew through her work on the SCU National Alumni Board. We made an appointment to meet with him. During the meeting, my mother asked him if he could do my grandfather and her a favor. She asked if he would be willing to accept me with only two years of a foreign language if I committed to taking one year of a foreign language my freshman year once I was admitted. Talk about your "presumptive close!" He reluctantly agreed.

Thanks to Mom and her relationship with the admissions director, I got accepted. I ended up taking

Italian my freshman year. I loved it so much that I spent a summer school session in Assisi, Italy, and eventually minored in Italian. My love for Italy and the language continues now almost thirty years later.

It's not always about what you know, but who you know. More broadly, it proves the value of building relationships. My mom was the queen of collecting relationships. Your relationships will help get you in the door. It then comes down to what you know that keeps you there.

Sales is all about building relationships. The real value is leveraging those relationships into future business. So to really grow your business, figure out who you know, so you can tell them what you know.

THE BEST SALESPEOPLE ARE FROM CHICO STATE

31

LEADERSHIP

My stepson, Charlie, has one of the most amazing memories of any person I have ever met. He can remember players name, the team he played for, and the score of a fourth-grade basketball game he played over ten years ago. It really is incredible. Because of his gift, he is the one who remembers and mimics my fortune cookie sayings the most. His memory is so good that he even reminds me of memories I have forgotten.

In preparation for writing this book, I asked Charlie to tell me his favorite fortune cookie line. His response was, "The best salespeople are from Chico State!" I found that to be funny. Of all the wisdom I have shared with him, this is the one? But maybe he was on to something.

California State University, Chico has been known for decades as a "party school." It is in a very small town in Northern California. My mother lived in Chico as a child. Her first-grade boyfriend from Chico is like an uncle, my Uncle Jimmy, to me today. I digress.

Because it is so secluded, the community of residents, faculty, and staff of Chico State have all melded together to form a great social environment for the students. The social interaction and the lack of a big city creates an opportunity for the students to really connect with one another. There are very few distractions. Therefore, the focus is on meeting new people and making new friends. Because Chico State is such a large school, meeting new people is just a way of life.

If you spent four years, from ages 18 to 22, constantly being introduced to new people, new communities, and new networks of people, how good would you be at cold calling? John Maxwell's book, *Failing Forward*, illustrates this point. "The less you venture out, the greater your risk of failure. Ironically the more you risk failure—and actually fail—the greater your chances of success."[1] By continually failing, you will lose your fear of failure. Once you lose your fear, you will start finding success.

When making your cold calls, the sooner you realize the *10,000 pound phone* won't actually kill you, the sooner and easier you will make them. Students and alumni from Chico State learn these valuable lessons early. They see the value in social interactions. They have suffered rejection and lived to tell about it.

Find a safe environment that allows you to learn and fail. It will eventually allow you to become your best. Be willing to set yourself up for failure, rejection, naysayers, and humiliation in order to ultimately reach your goals. Push yourself to make that one more call, appointment, foot canvas, or event. The more you fail, the less fear you will have of failure.

You know you will live to see another day. You will gain confidence in the losses and that will give you the strength to continue to your future successes.

I believe if you place yourself in an environment where you can learn from your failures and mistakes, your sense of confidence only increases. Chico State, and other schools like it, are a great environment for salespeople. There are no strangers . . . only friends we haven't yet met. Be proud, Wildcats. Chico State makes great salespeople.

NOTES

DAY BEFORE VACATION SYNDROME

32 LEADERSHIP

Since my oldest child, Kelsey, was born in 1998, I have worked every sort of mom schedule. You name it, I have done it. Part-time, job share, flex-time, full-time—it was all part of the ebb and flow of balancing my role as a mom and my passion to succeed profession-ally. Tricia Scalzo, my friend and former boss, hired me in 1999 when Kelsey was only a few months old.

The job was full-time, but I asked to only work three days a week. Tricia said that she felt I was overqualified for the job and would be successful, regardless of the hours. She and her boss were the only people in the company who knew I only worked three days a week. I thrived with the short work schedule and ended up being in the top ten percent of salespeople for the company.

Years later, I was the interim manager of a large real estate office of over 200 agents. The owner, Bev Steiner, wanted to see how I would manage the recruiting, profitability, training, coaching, and staff responsibilities of a large office while only working thirty hours per week. After six months, she offered the permanent position to me.

"I figured out how you are able to achieve your goals," she said. "Every day is like a day before vacation day for you."

You may have heard this before. It seems we all become just a little more efficient right before we go on vacation. We clean up our desks and clear out our email. We become more aware of our productivity management when it comes to taking meetings, scheduling calls, and answering the phone. It is amazing how much more efficient and effective we become when we are preparing to go on vacation.

So why can't we do that every day? You've heard the old adage, "The task fills the time allotted." If you don't set any time for a task, the task sets the time for you. When it is the day before vacation, you become diligent with your time, your calendar, and what tasks need to be completed before you head out of the office for a while.

In my manager job, I had to leave the office by 2 p.m. three days per week to pick up my kids from school. Two days a week, I worked until 5 p.m. Can you guess which days I was most effective? Yep! I seemed to get more accomplished on the shorter days.

Over time, I learned to calendar the longer days with more activities that needed to be done, but maybe weren't measurable activities. Fridays were my days to walk around the office, and to sit and chat with the staff, the salespeople, and vendors who came to see us. It was important to schedule time for relationships and connections in my office. If I didn't schedule the time, I could spend the afternoon doing nonproductive tasks such as checking email. More than once, I'd stop to send that one quick email, only to find out that an hour or two had passed without doing anything really productive or helpful for my agents. I hate that.

Now that my kids are older, they don't have to be picked up at 2:30 p.m. anymore. I still schedule a day or two a week to be finished by 3 p.m. so I can attend basketball games, grab a Jamba Juice, or just get caught up on the day with my teenagers.

Knowing I need to have my project for the day completed by 3 p.m., I become extremely efficient. Create a "day before vacation syndrome" for yourself. Simply have a start and end time every day. Put everything on your calendar—personal and professional. When you create times to accomplish your tasks and a finite time to complete them, you will be amazed how efficient you can be. So go ahead, you have my permission to make every tomorrow a vacation.

NOTES

IT IS BETTER TO BE OVERDRESSED THAN UNDERDRESSED

33 LEADERSHIP

My dad always told me it is better to be overdressed than underdressed for any occasion. He has also commented that *it* is better to be the best dressed person in the room than the worst dressed. I must have taken this a little too seriously. When I was nine years old, I bought my first suit. I had a briefcase, too!

My idol was this older lady (I now realize she was only twenty-five) who my parents had over for dinner. Her name was Cathy Fitzgerald. She was a salesperson who worked with my dad at Tandem Computers in the early 1980s. Cathy was smart, interesting, successful, and best of all for me, she was a professional salesperson! Until that moment, I didn't know selling things was a real job. I remember sitting and staring at her from across the dining room table and formulating the plan for my future career. I was totally drawn to the fact that she wore a suit. Cathy was dressed for success.

Dressing for success can have a lot of different connotations. Think about what you wear to a dinner party, to the gym, to work, or to a first date. Your clothes and how you present yourself are often people's first impression of you. Take pride in what you are wearing. Dressing for success doesn't always mean dressing in a suit and tie.

My daughter, Erika, was a big fan of *Fancy Nancy* and her tea parties years ago. What you wear to be successful at a tea party is different than what you wear to have a successful run or workout at the gym. A successful run requires athletic equipment: pants, shirt, sports bra, socks, shoes, and maybe a hat. Chuck loves to have his gear match, so he always has his Nike workout clothes coordinated. He has a sense of success before he ever steps foot into the gym.

Are you the best dressed person in your meetings at work? Do people notice how you present yourself? How do you feel when you are dressed well for an event? Are your clothes aligned with your goals of being successful, passionate, knowledgeable, and confident? Invest in a wardrobe that represents who you are and you will be surprised at the dividends it will pay. Dressing for success is the first step to truly being successful.

YOU CAN'T STEAL SECOND WITH YOUR FOOT STILL ON FIRST

If you haven't figured it out yet, I am a big baseball fan. As such, I was Coach Katey for my son's (Nathan's) Little League team. My son continues to focus on his dream of someday playing in MLB. Sounds good to me!

An important strategy in baseball is base stealing. Stealing second base is a combination of speed, risk, and timing. My favorite player, Rickey Henderson, is the all-time base stealing king. My dad was actually at the game when he broke the base stealing record, but I digress (if you couldn't tell, I could spend hours just writing about my passion for baseball).

What I love about the art of base stealing is that it is a calculated risk. It sort of falls in line with the "no guts, no glory" mindset. When coaching Little Leaguers about stealing, you not only have to train them on how to judge the ability and skill of the pitcher and catcher, but also to know their own ability, skill, and speed. However, maybe the most important thing in base stealing is something you can't always coach—the desire to go for it.

Successfully stealing a base usually puts your team in a better position to score. It can change the tempo of the game and force the other team to change their defensive strategy. Jackie Robinson, a prolific base stealer, would even steal home, which would give his team an extra run. Jackie and many all-time great base stealers have that "go for it" mindset to help their team.

Do you have a "go for it" attitude? Decide what calculated risks you are willing to take to put your team into a position to win. Whether you have sales, recruiting, mentoring, financial, or personal goals to meet, be willing to take the risks to make them happen. Sometimes that extra base will mean big success for your team. When you have little wins for your team, they compound into bigger opportunities for the entire team. It gives the team encouragement and excitement knowing that things are happening.

Like the runner on first, size up your competition. Decide if the risk is worth the reward. Decide if this opportunity can be leveraged into a success for you or your company. Make a decision when might be the proper time to "take that extra base."

Next, know your own abilities and capitalize on your strengths. If your skills aren't quite sharp enough, you may need to take some time to hone them. Work on things like lead generation and your presentation skills. If you aren't quite there yet, take some classes, hire a coach, seek out a mentor, or read this book again. If nothing else, just keep practicing.

Think about how many hours professional baseball players practice in relation to how many hours they play the game. During the season, on game day, professional baseball players arrive at the ballpark four to five hours before the first pitch. Professional baseball scouts come to watch players practice, warm up for the game, as well as how the player responds in game situations. We tend to play how we practice. When you are self-aware about your skill level, you can take the necessary steps to be ready.

The challenge is this: you cannot play it safe and expect to have exciting wins. The rush when you steal second base only happens because you took your foot off first and went for it. It is a calculated risk. Sometimes you will get thrown out. That's okay! Learn from it and move on to the next opportunity. Your passion for the win will help you get past those failures. You will never be 100 percent ready or 100 percent prepared to do all the necessary steps to take your foot off first base to head in the direction of your goals.

NOTES

LIFE IS ABOUT CHOICES

I remind my children on a regular basis that our lives are determined by the choices we make. I first heard this expression as a freshman at Carondelet High School in Concord, CA. We were the sister school to the all-boys, national power house, De La Salle High School. That year, the administration determined that we had lost our identity as strong young women so they closed the school for a day for us to refocus on who we were.

We broke into groups to discuss what actions we might take to rectify the situation. We also had a big rally with an inspirational speaker. The theme of this particular talk was "iCan." I cannot remember his name (yes, ironically it was a man), but he gave us each a lapel pin that was illustrated with a letter "i" in the middle of an aluminum can. It was a reminder that "I can" do anything.

In his speech, he told us that we can choose to do anything. He gave the example of going to school.

"You have a choice as to whether or not you go to school," he said. "You can choose not to go to school and then be picked up by a truancy officer and potentially go to juvenile hall. That is a choice. You choose to go to school because the alternative is less desirable than not going to school. Ultimately, it's a choice."

That stuck with me. Life is about choices. Our circumstances don't "happen to us." They are the sum of our choices. A bad grade doesn't "happen." It is often the result of a lack of commitment to studying or asking for help. My mom would hate it when, believe it or not, people would tell her she was *lucky* to be blessed with polite children. It wasn't luck at all. It was the result of my parents' commitment to daily discipline, setting limits for us at home, and teaching my sister and me acceptable behavior.

Yes, life events happen to each of us—both positive and negative. It seems to me that most of these events are far less frequent than the choices that lead up to the events. Many times, they are the results of acts of God (natural disasters), or the criminal, intentional, or negligent acts of others (getting run over in a crosswalk). When these life events do occur, we need to begin to make a choice about how we are going to handle them. Are we going to take positive action or sit around and wallow in a poor circumstance? Life is about choices.

The daily choices, habits, routines, and attitudes we display are the experiences we choose. Every day, we get the opportunity to choose. Choose your attitude. Choose your actions. Choose the life you want. When you wake up every day you can choose the life you want for yourself. Nothing in the past needs to influence what you do today. Just because you may have never run doesn't mean that today you don't strap on your sneakers and go for that jog. What choices are you making for yourself today?

NOTES

WORK SMARTER, NOT HARDER

36

LEADERSHIP

I have never been a fan of working hard. I am a fan of commitment, perseverance, challenging myself for personal growth, and the satisfaction of joyful exhaustion at the end of a day well spent in efforts to achieve my goals. Working hard always felt like a punishment. Working hard is what you do in high school to get through biology. It isn't fun. It is a finite time of drudgery. Why would anyone want to have a job that is "hard work"?

Instead, I believe in working smart. Maybe that is why I like being in sales. When I was twenty-eight, I was hired to sell national accounts for ADP. The VP for sales in California told me he didn't care if I worked from the moon, as long as I hit or beat my monthly and annual quota numbers. This was the same philosophy that helped me to be a top performing salesperson, working only three days a week when my daughter was a baby. In sales, we are judged and rewarded for our results, not the clock or even the methodology.

Working smart is about efficiencies, systems, and people. Efficiency can be that "day before vacation" mindset of working a shorter day or week to create a higher sense of urgency. Or tracking how you spend your time every day for a week to see where you can become more efficient. Implement a contact management system. Track your daily and weekly commitments. Time block your calendar. Leverage a part-time assistant to help you with your nonproductive tasks. Hire a business coach or meet with a mentor once a week to learn and grow. No need to reinvent the wheel. Learn from others. So start right now working smart, not hard!

WIN OR LEARN, NEVER LOSE

I am a competitor. Everything to me is a competition. When my sister, mom, and I would play cards, I would use every advantage to win the hand or the game. In most board games, the instructions include the rules of the game and how to play. I have never read the instructions in any game to learn how to win. The strategy to win is learned by playing the game, learning from others, and observation. Does this sound familiar? The strategy for how to be successful in business is learned the same way.

My son, Nathan, is also a competitor. He has always been that way. Nathan always wants to play a game, race someone, or challenge someone in trivia. When Nathan was in the fifth grade, he was playing Little League baseball and had already proven himself as an all-star. The team he was on had some kids who had never played baseball. As a pitcher, Nathan would pitch a great few innings, however the team would sometimes lose the game due to the inexperience of some of the new players. He would come off the field visibly frustrated. I could understand the frustration, but I wanted him to be a good teammate.

My friend and mentor, Nino Saso, gave me the best advice I ever heard for parents who have young athletes.

"When the game is over, the only thing you need to say to your kids is 'I love to watch you play,'" he said.

In fact, that should be the reason you are there—to watch the joy in your child's face when he or she plays a game he or she loves.

In Nathan's case, he wasn't loving the game. I have to admit, I was not happy with his attitude. So, after he had a minute to vent his frustration, I reminded him that they may not win a lot of games this season. Instead, it would be a season of learning. I decided to ask him some questions.

- Did you learn anything today?
- Did you watch someone make a great play and learn from it?
- Did you watch someone make a mistake and learn from it?
- Was there a previous lesson that was reinforced by your performance or the performance of one of your teammates?
- Did you learn how to be a better leader, to be more compassionate, to be a good friend?
- What lesson did you learn on the field today?
- If you lose the game and don't learn anything from it, then why play?

We can ask ourselves the same questions next time we have a loss or fail to get the results we expected. Losing doesn't feel good, however it is rarely fatal. How we feel about losing is a reminder of how badly we want to win, it tests our commitment to getting better, and is a reminder of how much more we need to do to get the result we want.

Failure is part of playing any game. In sales, we win and lose clients, negotiations, and opportunities. We need to learn from each loss. There is a long list of great political, business, entertainment, and sports icons who have failed, learned from their mistakes, and gone on to achieve great things.

Commit to assessing and learning from your mistakes, failures, and losses. Whether you want to be a top salesperson, a Hall of Fame baseball player, or just take a great vacation, stay focused on your dreams. If you continue to learn, all your dreams can become realities. Keep failing; it is the best teacher. Win or learn, never lose.

NOTES

TRYING IS FAILING WITH HONOR

I *hate* the word "try." Maybe it is because I am a sci-fi geek and watch *Star Wars* too often.

"Do or do not," Yoda says. "There is no try."

Or maybe it is because I have heard mentors tell me that *try* doesn't really mean anything.

"*Try* to pick up this pen. You can't. You either pick up the pen or you don't."

Maybe it is the fallback word people use when they don't want you to feel bad or hold them accountable to their choices.

"I tried to make it to your party."

"I tried to clean up my room."

"I tried to eat healthy."

I don't know why people use it. I do know that my children are not allowed to use the word *try* in my presence.

One expression I like to use with my kids is, "Trying is failing with honor." I love that! Using the word *try* somehow makes us feel like we didn't fail. But we did. I use this phrase a lot. When I coach salespeople, I do not let them use the word *try* as part of the accountability process. What are you going to commit to doing this week, month, or year? The word *try* doesn't tell me or you what needs to be done to meet your goals. At the end of the year, you either hit your goals or you don't.

When my son Nathan was seven, he asked me what he is supposed to say instead of *try* when he is learning a new skill.

"I am doing my best."

Nathan's coaches have often remarked at the use of this phrase in his athletic career. Giving your best to any task, new skill, or your team is all we can ask of ourselves and each other. Are you committed to giving your best? Are you willing to be honest with yourself on achieving your daily tasks to meet your short-term and long-term goals? What will you commit to doing? "Do or do not. There is no *try*!"

WHAT IS YOUR HOURLY RATE?

When I use this "fortune cookie" line, my intention is to send a message about leverage. I also use it to determine how you prioritize your time. Gary Keller once said, "If you don't hire a gardener, you are one." Make the best use of the twenty-four hours that you are given every day.

In real estate sales, the best example I have is when a real estate agent wants to control the process, the clients, the vendors, affiliates, and the paperwork. Attempting to control every aspect of the job is not the best use of one's time. Every office will likely have at least one person who spends 100 percent of his or her time working on the paperwork aspect of real estate. These amazing people are called transaction coordinators (TC). My all-time favorite TC is Katie Maria. She was so good that she started her own company to increase efficiencies for her team and her clients.

My point is, when a real estate agent manages the paperwork on a file, it can sometimes take six hours or more over the course of a transaction. A fantastic TC can usually manage the process in less than four hours. In those same six hours, a real estate agent could be finding another client.

In the San Francisco Bay area, the average fee for a TC is about $500. The average commission check for REALTOR® in that area is $15,000, or more. So, to truly maximize production, do you think salespersons need to be doing paperwork or finding new clients? Their hourly rate is significantly increased if they spend those hours searching for new business rather than doing the paperwork on the ones they already have.

The objection I often get from real estate agents and loan officers I have consulted over the years is, "But my clients only want to work with me!"

"The last time you went to KFC, did the Colonel make your chicken?" I often ask.

Of course *he* didn't make the chicken! He's been dead for years. Amazingly, we are still able to get the same great chicken without the Colonel being there. How is that possible? The Colonel simply managed the process and standards so that the client still gets that finger lickin' goodness, even though the Colonel is no longer cooking the chicken himself.

I believe the same is true in sales. Your clients love you, of course, and they expect a certain quality of service. Your job is to provide them with the same or better customer experience while still leveraging your time. When you choose to have someone help you with supporting your clients, you have to manage the process and standards, not every detail. Typically, when you hire a specialist, as in the example of a TC, he or she can do it better than you can. I know my cleaning service cleans my house better than I do!

Specialists have a much higher hourly rate than generalists. That is true in any industry. Become a specialist in finding and helping your current and future customers. Paperwork, repeatable documents, and certain procedures can either be automated or outsourced to a specialist. Find the area where you are the specialist. Maximize your time there. When it comes to everything else, give it to someone who can do it better than you. Increase your expertise in your specialty area and watch your hourly rate soar!

NOTES

CHANGE CREATES OPPORTUNITY

People hate change. Well maybe they don't really hate it. They just fear it. However, the reality is that if we don't change, we die. Stagnant waters breed death and/or pestilence. Rivers are a constant source of change. Over time, flowing water, with its consistent power and persistence, can change the shape of rock. It is therefore my belief that change creates opportunity. You just need to be ready to take advantage of the opportunity when change happens.

In 2007, the real estate market "bubble" burst. Movies were made that showed the financial devastation. Laws were enacted to prevent or minimize the potential of it from happening again. Leading up to 2007, the real estate market was a definite seller's market. It was the purest form of supply and demand at work. Short inventory, lots of income, and low barrier to get a loan made for high demand. The opportunity for sellers to cash in on this amazing opportunity was great.

Then the credit crisis occurred and there was a *huge* change. Obviously, many people were negatively affected by the bursting of the real estate bubble. However, it also created great opportunity. Willing buyers, who had been shut out or outbid in the previous few years, were finally able to buy those same homes at a discounted price. Opportunity was also created for investors to purchase property, as well as for property management companies who were overloaded with former home owners now needing to rent. In every market, there is an opportunity, but for whom?

When companies merge, when a new employer comes to town, when your boss retires, or when your youngest child goes off to college, an opportunity is created. You just need to figure out what that opportunity is and who will benefit from it. Be willing to ask questions. Find out what the need is and see if there is a problem to solve. Change creates opportunity. So, the next time you see a change coming, make sure to make it an opportunity that benefits you, your team, or your clients.

DEAD RIGHT

Occasionally, my mom used to sit in a car at an intersection and say "dead right." Imagine the following scenario: You are sitting in your car at a red light, waiting for the light to turn green. As it does, you let your foot off the brake, only to have another car come flying across your path through the intersection at Mach 2. You slam on your brakes. You had the right of way, but decided to let the low-flying jet on wheels go ahead of you. You have probably heard the quote, "Discretion is the better part of valor." Had you stood on the principle of being right, you might also be dead.

In every aspect of our life, we have those moments when we know we are absolutely right. The problem is, sometimes being right doesn't lead to the absolute best outcome. So you have to ask yourself what is more import to you: being right or reaching a mutually beneficial result?

In marriage, we often hear the question, "Would you rather be right or happy?" We all have had those discussions with our spouse when we know we are totally in the right. We also know if we stick to our guns, we will be sleeping on the couch.

In business or sales, "the customer is always right." Those of us who have been around long enough know that isn't true. However, in order to save a client or transaction, we swallow our pride and determine that the long-term relationship is more important than being right in that particular moment.

This is also true in many negotiations. Often, it is about perspective. By thinking creatively, we start to look for opportunities versus road blocks. You need to decide the greater right. If you are right and it kills the deal, is that really right?

It may be that both sides can be "right" and refuse to budge due to conviction. In this case, one or both of the parties needs to change perspective and ask "How do we make this work?" As discussed in chapter 29, sometimes we just need to agree to disagree.

When you find yourself in this kind of standoff, step back and evaluate your ultimate goal. By doing so, you can begin to think more creatively. You might find that even more opportunities exist. You may have to change your definition of what is right. Is being right taking care of the needs of your client, closing the transaction, maintaining your integrity, or gaining the trust of a new relationship? Only you can define what is "right" in any situation.

Being right doesn't always mean winning. Sometimes, it can mean living to fight another day. Define what is truly right for you and your client so you can win the deal, maintain the relationship, and own your integrity. Next time, put your ego in check so you don't end up being "dead right."

NOTES

SEXY, BUT NOT SLUTTY

42

LEADERSHIP

For years, I have been going to Fusion 3 Salon, in Pleasanton, CA, to get my haircut. Although I go to the same salon, the same person doesn't always cut my hair. Therefore, the stylist will ask me how I want my hair. My standard response is, "Sexy, but not slutty." That usually gets a big laugh from anyone in earshot.

Although it may sound funny, it is true! I want to exude that look of attractiveness, confidence, intelligence, success, and charisma. Those are the qualities I find sexy. The "not slutty" part is that fine line that moves from confidence to desperation. Desperate is *not* sexy.

In my career, I have warned that a desperate salesperson, in any field, is not sexy. It is commonly known as "commission breath." Commission breath is the worst case of halitosis. It is that lack of quality and/or integrity in which you are willing to do or say almost anything to make the sale and "earn" your commission.

I will admit sex sells. This is not new information. Just ask Carl's Jr. with their supermodel campaign. I laugh when I see a TV commercial that insinuates that you can "get the girl," be more attractive to others, or "get lucky" if you just buy the right perfume, deodorant, or car.

But what is sexy? Sexy, like beauty, is often in the eye of the beholder. I have met men who are physically very sexy, but then they start talking. Oh, no! The more they talk, the less sexy they get. I have also met men who have an average look, but when they start talking, wow! The sexy meter goes way up! So sexy isn't always about just looks.

People magazine has an annual "sexiest man alive" issue. Chuck claims to always be in the running (maybe someday, baby). Of course, these men are physically attractive, but that is not the only thing that makes them sexy. In my humble opinion, sexy is:

- Confident
- Intelligent
- Humble
- Smart
- Funny
- Strong (emotionally and physically)
- Sensitive
- Honorable
- Vulnerable
- Gracious

I'm sure you have your own list. For me, these are also the attributes of a gentleman. My son has been opening doors and pulling out chairs for ladies since he was five years old. Chivalry is not going to die on my watch! The above attributes can also apply to women. Chivalry is like a dance between a lady and a gentleman. It is built on mutual respect and trust. If either neglects the qualities of being a lady or gentleman, the dance fails.

You are probably asking by now, how does this put money in my pocket? Simple . . . be sexy! When you exude sexy attributes, it is attractive to clients. They will be drawn to you. You will not have to be desperate to seek them. Desperate is *not* sexy! So be smart, confident, humble, gracious, and honest. Show up every day being solution-oriented and willing to help people. Be sexy, not slutty.

NOTES

A MENTOR'S HINDSIGHT IS YOUR FORESIGHT

43 LEADERSHIP

In chapter 33, I introduced you to my dad's co-worker, Cathy Fitzgerald. She was the top salesperson at Tandem Computers, which, at the time, was a small startup. In my eyes, Cathy was a rock star.

My dad was in sales support. Once the sales team had identified an opportunity and done an initial needs analysis, the sales support team would come in to make sure the technical aspects of the transactions were done right.

When I was nine, we had Cathy over for dinner. Even though I had been a top salesperson since the first-grade, I was totally in awe of her. It was the first time I realized that my talents as a salesperson could be a real job. Cathy was the embodiment of what I wanted to be when I grew up. She arrived at our house wearing a gorgeous suit. She was smart, beautiful, funny, interesting, and successful. My parents treated her like family and she is still a part of our lives today.

At that moment, Cathy became a mentor for me. I bought my first suit at the age of nine and haven't looked back. My parents kept me informed of Cathy's successes, opportunities to further her career, and personal accomplishments. Cathy and I have met several times over my life and her insight is always appreciated. She is a success in multiple aspects of her life, both professionally and personally. I still look forward to her Christmas card, which reminds me, I need to spend more time with her. Many of my dreams and aspirations came from seeing Cathy accomplish so many things.

I tell you this story because hindsight is 20/20. Find someone whose hindsight can serve as your foresight. If you want to be a top producing salesperson, go spend time with top producing salespeople. If you want to learn how to invest in real estate, go meet with people who are already doing it. If you want to write a book, meet with people who have written books. The saying goes: "The smart person learns from his/her mistakes; the wise person learns from the smart person's mistakes." Why make your own mistakes when someone has already made those mistakes? Learn from him or her.

I have never been a fan of reinventing the wheel. If someone has already done it, follow the recipe. Once you follow the recipe a few times, then you can go and put your own style or spin on it. The basics of success leave clues. The majority of what successful people have done or not done can be emulated by you. In areas in which I have had a mentor, I have been very purposeful. When I have failed to have a mentor, I have struggled.

Do you have a mentor? When you find a mentor who can guide you in the direction you want to go, there is nothing better. He or she can become a friend, a confidant, and a sounding board. A good one will even be willing to kick you in the rear every once in a while.

Are you a mentor? The best way to learn is to teach. As important as it is to have a mentor, it is equally important to be a mentor. The days of the "old boys club" can live on with one mentoring relationship at a time. The concept of the old boys club is significant because those associations allowed for members to share wisdom, guide one another, and lift each other to succeed at the next level. They are a great example of taking someone under your wing to guide and teach that person how to be successful. Be clear on where you want to go, then find someone who has already been there. That person's hindsight is your foresight.

On the TV show *The West Wing* Leo tells Josh the following story (Josh refers to it when talking to Leo in "Barlet for America"):

> *"This guy's walking down the street when he falls in a hole. The walls are so steep he can't get out.*
> *"A doctor passes by and the guy shouts up, 'Hey you. Can you help me out?' The doctor writes a prescription, throws it down in the hole and moves on.*
> *"Then a priest comes along and the guy shouts up, 'Father, I'm down in this hole can you help me out?' The priest writes out a prayer, throws it down in the hole and moves on.*

"Then a friend walks by, 'Hey, Joe, it's me can you help me out?' And the friend jumps in the hole. Our guy says, 'Are you stupid? Now we're both down here.' The friend says, 'Yeah, but I've been down here before and I know the way out.'"[1] Joe is the perfect mentor to help our guy find his way out of the hole. Find your "Joe" to help you find your eay to your goals. A mentor's hindsight can be your foresight."

BE COMFORTABLE BEING UNCOMFORTABLE

44

LEADERSHIP

When Erika was twelve years old, she was struggling with challenges at school because of her dyslexia. Dealing with middle school, puberty, and the intense amount of effort it took for her to go to school was exhausting. I shared with her this story . . .

Once a little boy was playing outdoors and found a fascinating caterpillar. He carefully picked it up and took it home to show his mother. He asked his mother if he could keep it, and she said he could if he would take good care of it.

The little boy got a large jar from his mother and put plants to eat, and a stick to climb on, in the jar. Every day he watched the caterpillar and brought it new plants to eat.

One day the caterpillar climbed up the stick and started acting strangely. The boy worriedly called his mother who came and understood that the caterpillar was creating a cocoon. The mother explained to the boy how the caterpillar was going to go through a meta-morphosis and become a butterfly.

The little boy was thrilled to hear about the changes his caterpillar would go through. He watched every day, waiting for the butterfly to emerge. One day, it happened—a small hole appeared in the cocoon and the butterfly started to struggle to come out.

At first, the boy was excited, but soon he became concerned. The butterfly was struggling so hard to get out! It looked like it couldn't break free! It looked desperate! It looked like it was making no progress!

The boy was so concerned that he decided to help. He ran to get scissors, and then walked back (because he had learned not to run with scissors). He snipped the cocoon to make the hole bigger and the butterfly quickly emerged!

As the butterfly came out, the boy was surprised. It had a swollen body and small, shriveled wings. He continued to watch the butterfly, expecting that at any moment, the wings would dry out, enlarge, and expand to support the swollen body. He knew that in time the body would shrink and the butterfly's wings would expand. But neither happened!

The butterfly spent the rest of its life crawling around with a swollen body and shriveled wings. It never was able to fly.

As the boy tried to figure out what had gone wrong, his mother took him to talk to a scientist from a local college. He learned that the butterfly was supposed to struggle. In fact, the butterfly's struggle to push its way through the tiny opening of the cocoon pushes the fluid out of its body and into its wings. Without the struggle, the butterfly would never, ever fly. The boy's good intentions hurt the butterfly.[1]

We then discussed how the struggle that feels tough in the moment is often what gives us the tools to be successful. The struggle ultimately makes us strong and helps give us confidence to take on the next challenge.

A few days after telling Erika the story, I offered to help her with a project that she was having difficulty completing. Erika looked at me and said, "Mom, I got this. Don't cut my cocoon! I am becoming a butterfly." It made me laugh with a great sense of pride. At the ripe old age of twelve, Erika understood what many professional salespeople do not: that struggle and being uncomfortable is what ultimately makes us strong.

Both personally and professionally, I look at the combination of struggles and successes as part of a beautiful quilt that is my life. My successes are the prettier and more colorful pieces. They always seem to shine more brightly when I view them in contrast to my struggles and hardships represented by the darker pieces.

For whatever reason, we tend to learn more from our failure than our success. Our struggles take us from good to great. The times of learning, struggle, and discomfort are what give us the knowledge, strength, and confidence to take the next step.

Look for opportunities to be uncomfortable. Get out of your comfort zone. Training for a marathon is uncomfortable. The feeling of triumph when you cross the finish line, regardless of the time, is worth every second of the struggle. Learning a new language can often be very difficult. However, the feeling of confidently navigating your travel in a foreign country is fun and empowering. Negotiating a tough transaction can often be painstaking. Achieving a win-win outcome in which you create a lasting, successful, and profitable relationship is not only rewarding in the moment but gives you confidence to go after the next tough transaction, because you have done it before.

When looking back at those uncomfortable times in my life—the death of my mother, divorce, debt, weight gain, professional challenges—I came away with a stronger and deeper understanding of myself. I learned and grew from my struggles. The most important lesson I learned from all of them is that my fear of failure diminished. Since I have experienced struggle and persevered to success, I know I have the skills, knowledge, and mindset to take on whatever is set before me, no matter how uncomfortable.

Michael Regan, my business coach, tells me to "lean in" to both the struggles and opportunities. Learning to lean into the uncomfortable experiences is what helps to decrease fear, build confidence, and create our own version of the butterfly within ourselves. Be comfortable being uncomfortable. Be willing to push your wings against the sides of your cocoon. Only then will you truly be released to become your own beautiful and unique butterfly.

NOTES

GO FOR NO!

Years ago, a fellow salesperson gave me a great book called *Go for No!* by Richard Fenton and Andrea Waltz.[1] It illustrated how successful you can be if you are able to overcome your self-limiting beliefs and fear of failure. It showed how hearing the word "no" doesn't have to be a negative concept, that it can actually be empowering and motivating. Get enough no's and you end up with a map to a yes.

Whether I was selling copiers, payroll services, or houses, I would foot canvas. Foot canvassing is when you knock on doors, either in an office building, strip mall, or residential area to find new potential clients. I was the master of ignoring the "no soliciting" sign. I perfected the art of just asking a few questions to discover whether a person had any need or interest in my services.

As you can probably imagine, I received a lot of rejections, and I also got a lot of appointments, too.

People seemed to like looking me in the eye, feeling my energy, and listening to what I had to say. The key to much of my success was looking people in the eye. It is always tougher to say no to someone face to face than over the phone. Being somewhat naïve yet very optimistic, my perspective on the rejection was that receiving a no wasn't a failure, but instead it meant "not now," and was therefore an opportunity for the future. I never took no as a personal rejection of me. It was just a sign that it wasn't the right time for my service or product. After a while, I could determine how many no responses I would get before getting to a yes. Soon it was a game to keep track of the "no" responses because I knew that each "no" got me closer to a "Yes!"

Why do we get so caught up with rejection? We get rejected by those closest to us on a daily basis. Our kids reject our requests. Our spouses reject our ideas. Our parents reject our choices. If we get rejected daily by the people closest to us, and don't seem to mind it, then why would we fear getting rejected by perfect strangers?

Ask for their business. It's okay if they say no. Remember, "no" may just mean "not right now." We don't ask because we fear the answer (see chapter 1 *Closed Mouths Don't Get Fed*). I'm speculating that part of our fear is the reason we got into sales in the first place. We are people persons. We enjoy interacting with others. If those same people are saying no to us, it stings a little. We all want to be liked and accepted. To get over our fears, we need to change our mindset.

What if your job as a lead generation machine was just to introduce people to your product or service? They don't actually have to buy it. Would that make it easier for you to approach them? Take the approach that all you are doing is educating your prospective clients. Give them information to make an informed decision. Some people will still say no, but who cares? Move on to the next. There are seven billion people in the world.

Truth be told, I would rather get a no than a maybe. A maybe sends a message of ambiguity. There is no sense of win or learn (see chapter 37). I'm stuck wondering whether this person is worth more effort. If I get a no, I can ask the client what his or her objections are and learn from them. I can then either come up with solutions to overcome the objections or simply move on, realizing this particular client isn't an opportunity. Once again, sales is all about production management. Is this "maybe" client worth my time and effort?

Keep track of how many no responses you need to get to yes. Then you will look forward to the no, knowing you are one step closer to the people who need or want your product or service. Make a game out of it. Keep moving and have fun! Sales is a contact sport and some of those contacts will be "No" . . . for now! So keep going for it!

NOTES

SALES GOALS ARE JUST A ROAD TRIP

46
LEADERSHIP

I live in the San Francisco Bay Area. My dad's family is from the Chicago area. I look at business planning like a road trip from San Francisco to Chicago. It is a similar process. Have a starting place, have a destination, and have a timeline for how quickly you want to be there. Then break the process down to bite size pieces.

- In a car, leave San Francisco, California
  - o Get on US-101 S (3 minutes, 0.6 miles)
  - o Follow I-80 E and I-88 E to W Congress Pkwy in Chicago (30 hours, 2,131 miles) – stop to sleep in Salt Lake City, Utah, and Omaha, Nebraska
  - o Continue on W Congress Pkwy and drive to S Federal St (3 minutes, 0.5 miles)
- Arrive Chicago, Illinois

You know your starting and ending point, as well as the route you plan to travel. Now you just have to figure out your pace. The entire trip, taking 80 East, is a little over 2,100 miles. If you did the trip in three days, you would be driving about twelve hours per day. That's a lot of driving each day. If you stretched your trip over a week, you could build in some stops along the way to enjoy the adventures. The week-long trip might even be better for your health. Of course, if you were in a real hurry, you could fly. The point is, business planning is just like trip planning. Set your course for your goal and the speed at which you want to arrive and then get moving.

If hitting your financial goals quickly is a priority, there might be some discomfort. You will need to be very focused on the road ahead and be willing to commit to the discipline it will take to get you there fast. If your goals are more long-term, you still need to be committed but maybe just not so aggressive. Either plan is great. It is up to you.

Decide your destination (your goals) and when you want to arrive. Then use your map (business plan) to decide the route you want to take. It then becomes simple math.

Here is an example for a REALTOR®:

1. Financial goal for the year ($250,000)
2. An average commission check for one house sold is $10,000
3. Example of $250,000 divided by $10,000, would be 25 transactions needed to meet the annual goal
4. Annual goals to make $250,000

- 25 transactions
- 100 appointments (assume 25% of appointment to closed transaction)
- 400 leads (assume 25% of leads convert to appointments)

5. Weekly Goals
    a. Weeks worked per year
        i. 40 weeks working in your business
        ii. 12 weeks out of your business
            1. Vacation
            2. Trainings
            3. Biz planning (once per quarter)
    b. 1-2 transactions bi-weekly to meet goal
    c. 2 appointments per week to meet goal
    d. 10 leads per week to meet goal
6. Go Do It!

Set your goal. Make your road map. Fill out your calendar with the activities to get you where you want to be. And enjoy your trip!

NOTES

COMPOUND EFFECT

47

LEADERSHIP

Darren Hardy's book, *The Compound Effect*, had a significant impact on my life.[1] The basic idea of the book is that small incremental commitments or choices can impact your life in a large way. It can work in both the positive and the negative.

An example would be your daily diet and exercise routine. A few extra calories consumed than you burn every day turn into a few extra unwanted pounds every year on your body. A few more calories burned than consumed turn into losing those few unwanted pounds every year.

It is not rocket science. Often, the simplest things we do are also the most challenging. It is no different in the business world. One more call, one more appointment, or one more proposal sent out each day or week can turn into very big returns over the course of a year.

I am Catholic, so I feel guilty about everything. Sometimes, after knowing I have made a bad choice, I get that feeling in the pit of my stomach. It is that sense of knowing I have made a poor decision. In the year after my divorce, I made a lot of those type choices. I have come to find out that it is apparently quite common for a recent divorcee to have a second adolescence and act out like an indignant teenager. In most aspects, I am far from common. In regard to my post-divorce behavior, I was very much part of the crowd.

I remember waking up in the middle of night after a night of drinking with my friends and wondering how I got home. I panicked and ran to the garage. Sure enough, there was my car. I had driven home and didn't remember it. That sinking feeling in the pit of my stomach was unbearable. The repercussions to the custody of my children, and the possible loss of my career and my personal security overwhelmed me. I started thinking about how many times I had made a wrong decision, one after the other. At that moment, I started to make right choices to never have that feeling again.

One of those choices was to curtail my alcohol consumption. I now have a commitment that I don't drink for the first quarter of each New Year. My kids became my accountability partners. They are amazingly helpful. I also shared my commitment to a healthier lifestyle with my friends. Instead of alcohol, green tea and Pellegrino became my drink of choice.

The compounded effect was remarkable. It seems that many of my poor food choices were connected to alcoholic drinks. By choosing Pellegrino, I ate better, slept better, and felt better getting up for my morning walks. The ripple effect gave me perspective on a whole variety of simple choices that made huge impacts on my life. I made healthier choices in food, exercise, and relationships. At work, I made wiser choices. The positives kept building on themselves. In those three months, I lost about ten pounds and had renewed energy and motivation.

My first quarter prohibition is a reminder of where I have been and how strong I am now to make my life anything I want it to be. I understand that I have failed. I know that I have made huge mistakes. I also have learned that small choices can lead to huge positive successes. I have survived and I have thrived.

The first quarter prompts me to keep perspective. It also reminds me that failure is not the end. Failure is just a place to start again and choose wisely. A little choice each day in a positive direction will make significant impacts on your life.

The sales lesson here is to just do one more. Make one more call a day. Knock on just one more door each day. Take one more class each month. Each one adds up. You can do the math. You know what you need to do for your business to be successful. Start today.

NOTES

ENTHUSIASM SELLS

In 1991, I took a job at The Sharper Image in the mall. The Sharper Image store was featured in a scene in the movie *When Harry Met Sally*. It was a store full of all sorts of gadgets and grownup toys. I was hired to sell gel insole products, solely as a demonstrator. My commission was 100 percent based on the sale of insoles and nothing else in the store.

My station was near the entrance of the store that faced the interior of the mall. I had three chairs set up so people could put the insoles into their shoes and walk around the store to see if they liked them. After doing so, some said "it was like having a baby waterbed on my feet," and others said, "I felt like I was walking in wet sand." Some people loved them. Others didn't care for them at all. I learned a lot more about people's feet and how people thought about their feet than I needed or wanted to hear.

My job was exclusively to persuade people to come into the store, try on the insoles, hope they liked them, and make the sale. This may have been how I learned that it was my job to create an opportunity and not be tied to the outcome. People generally either liked them right away or hated them instantly. It wasn't about me at all.

My "sole" (insole humor) focus was getting people in the door. To do so, I had to create some sense of excitement. I decided that my pitch was going to be, "Want to come in and get a massage for your feet?" I stood facing the mall and made sure I was excited. If I was excited about the foot massage, people would come into the store. If I was tired or upset, my energy dropped and so would the number of people who came into the store. It became obvious that my sales were directly tied to my enthusiasm.

Enthusiasm, energy, and excitement can be contagious. You need to be enthusiastic about what you do. If you aren't excited about what you do, how can you expect anyone else to be? If you are enthusiastic and excited about what you are doing, other people will be naturally attracted to it.

When I coach real estate agents, I often hear, "I don't like to do open houses." My response is generally, "Then don't do them!" Why would you ever do a lead generation technique that you didn't like? Often, sales isn't about what you say, but how you and your body say it. Communication is not only about your words, but your tone and energy. When you are excited about what you do and how well you do it, other people will be attracted to you and be interested in what you are selling.

Find the aspect of your job that excites you, inspires you, and brings you joy. Create the opportunity to share your product or service by sharing your enthusiasm for what you do. Part of being in sales is to create an experience. Make sure that experience has some enthusiasm in it, because enthusiasm sells!

NOTES

ARE YOU A GUNSLINGER OR A SNIPER?

49

LEADERSHIP

I want to suggest that there are two types of salespeople. One I'll call a gunslinger, the other I'll call a sniper. In the old western TV shows, gunslingers would saunter into a room or down the street and rely on their instincts and speed to win the battle. They would come up against a challenger and just open fire, fast and furious. Often, they didn't even hit where they were aiming. In many instances, they didn't fare very well by literally shooting from the hip.

Snipers, on the other hand, are meticulous in their preparation. They spend as much time as they can, measuring and practicing everything before they take the shot. Snipers may only take one shot. More often than not, it's going to be right on target.

Most of us have a little of each in us. It often depends on time and context. Sometimes, you need the gunslinger on short notice. Those are the times when taking immediate action is the priority. You just need to get a job done. It isn't important for it to be neat and perfect. Other times, precision and perfection are required.

When crafting your business plan, decide what method will be most effective. It may be one or the other or a combination of both. As discussed in chapter 14 (DISC), we all have our different behavioral styles. When creating your team, decide what combination of gunslingers and snipers you need to be most effective.

Personally, I tend to be more of a gunslinger, along the lines of the Sundance Kid. My sister, Karolyn, is more of a sniper. Karolyn is a natural planner, strategist, and analyst. Her first job was as an analyst that helped to guide satellites. Karolyn tends to measure twice and cut once. She is a careful planner who makes sure that every detail is taken care of and every item on the instruction guide is mastered. I generally just hit buttons on the computer until I get the desired result. I use my gut to make decisions.

Gunslingers tend to be more tacticians. Snipers tend to be more strategists. In many ways, we need each other. Gunslingers typically make decisions quickly, though not always accurately. Snipers make decisions more slowly, though tend to be more accurate. There are advantages and disadvantages to both.

In sales, we need to have a little bit of both. If you are a gunslinger, schedule a part of your week to do some sniper work, like thinking and planning. If you are a sniper, schedule time to quickly check items off your list. It is good to know what kind of salesperson you are. Your clients will appreciate you for your natural talents. When you are aware of what you bring to the negotiation, sales presentation, or meeting, you will bring your best self. If you do, you will hit your target.

NOTES

FRICTION MAKES THE FIRE

I am very proud of my ancestry. On my dad's side, I get my Italian from the Dallostos and the Milanis. On my mom's side, I get my Irish from the Carrs and Kennedys. What this means to me is that not only do I love a good fight, but I like it loud.

Often, when Chuck and I are having a "discussion," our kids get a little uncomfortable and will tell us so. My standard response is, "Friction makes the fire," which generally just adds to their discomfort. It is sort of like tigers playing. The tigers are having a great time and everyone else is a bit scared.

I love the expression on a couple different levels. The first is that there is a component of passion, which is a good thing. We all need a little passion in our lives. The second is the concept that we all need a little conflict or friction in our lives to allow us to grow.

Former secretary of state, Condoleezza Rice, spoke at Santa Clara University. She was asked what one piece of advice she would give to a college student. Without hesitation, she said, "If your friends are always agreeing with you or telling you that you are always right, then you need to get a new set of friends." She went on to explain that it is only with healthy disagreement and discussion that we expand our thinking. If you are the best dressed, smartest, highest paid, most spiritual, and/or doing the most community service in your group of friends, then you need new friends.

The same goes for us in business. If we aren't constantly and consistently being challenged or pushed, we will become stagnant in our growth. In *The Five Dysfunctions of a Team* by Patrick Leniconi, conflict is identified as one of the key attributes of a successful and functional team. I think of conflict like harmonies in music. The conflict between different sounds, voices, and tempo is what makes it great and powerful.

Why conflict or friction? As in music, different voices give us a more rounded way of thinking. We gain perspective. Different voices give us opportunities to grow and open our minds to new ideas and possibilities. Positive friction in business helps companies make better decisions by weighing all the possibilities. Without the friction, things can get a little boring, single-minded, and can lead to making bad decisions.

Surround yourself with people and mentors who create a little bit of friction for you. Once, I was frustrated that I was spending time waiting for things to happen that were entirely out of my control. I shared my frustration and impatience with my friend and mentor, Keith Robinson. Keith told me, "You suck at waiting." It was a tiny bit of friction that challenged me to do something that was in my control. It prompted me to stop waiting for things to happen *to* me. I took control of my actions and surroundings and began to *make* things happen. That was actually the spark that lit the fire that helped me finish this book. Fire is good. It can create enough steam to power a locomotive.

Good friction can help a team be more successful. It can help us to grow and be better versions of ourselves. It can even heat up some passion in our relationships. You need to have the attitude of "I love you enough to want to make you better." So, go ahead and create as much friction as possible, so you too can catch fire in your career.

NOTES

I'M STILL HERE

My sister, Karolyn, read this poem at our Mom's memorial service.

I won't be far away,
For life goes on
So if you need me, call
And I will come.
Though you cannot see or touch me,
I'll be near
And if you listen with your heart,
You'll hear all of my love around you soft and clear
And then,
When you must come this way alone
I'll greet you with a smile,
And say, "Welcome Home"[1]

My mom beat stage 4 lymphoma in 1997, but eventually lost her life to pneumonia in February 1998. I was in her hospital room just before she passed away. Mom's hospital room became the space where friends and family gathered. It became like a small vigil for her. At the time, I was five months pregnant with Kelsey. Kelsey was to be my first child and my mother's first grandchild. Kelsey's middle name is Ann to honor my mom. The day I learned that my mom was dying was also the same day I had my ultrasound when I found out my new baby was going to be a girl. Talk about an emotional roller coaster.

During our little vigil, Mom had lots of visitors and friends stop by to see her, make her laugh, and tell stories. Between visitors, Mom napped. We all took turns by her bed. We couldn't help but cry. Once, when it was my dad's turn, Mom woke up. She looked at Dad and said, "I'm still here." We all giggled a bit.

My mom is still here in so many ways. After she died, I was scared to have a baby without her. Even though I was saddened by her death, I felt blessed to have this new life inside me. It seemed like every time I was crying or upset, Kelsey would give me a little kick to remind me that my mom was still here.

Kelsey is still the one who checks in on me around my mom's birthday or on the anniversary of her death. She has such a kind soul. My mom is still here with her.

Mom is also still here in the spirit of two wonderful friends of hers: Ann Manchester and Gloria Pearce. They both helped me when Kelsey was born. I was living in Hawaii at the time. Ann arrived in Honolulu on Kelsey's due date. However, Kelsey was ten days late, so we had lots of fun on the beaches of Oahu despite the fact that I was huge. Ann was there for three weeks and helped me with the emotional, physical, and mental aspects of having my first child. Ann and her husband, Jeff, live nearby now and continue to be a wonderful part of our extended family. My kids even affectionately refer to her as "Ann 2." Mom was first. Mom is still here.

Gloria Pearce and her husband, Bud, came out for a week when Kelsey was about a month old. They are the parents of six children. If you ever need to learn about how to "not sweat the small stuff," spend time with the parents of six children. It was awesome. Gloria is a straight shooter and very direct. She is also an amazing cook and kept me well-fed. Her style of a little tough love and perspective were exactly what I needed whenever I started to feel sorry for myself. Mom is still here.

The principal at my kids' school was a friend and student of Mom's. I continue to meet people on a regular basis who were friends or students of hers. Of course, everyone Mom met ended up being her friend.

My mom is still here in the funny way Erika tilts her head and smiles with her dimple showing and eyes shimmering. Mom is still here in Nathan's skin-tone and tender heart. Mom is still here even in Chuck, who never met Mom, when he says and does things Mom said and did. Her spirit lives on. Mom is still here.

So, what is the leadership lesson? We can all learn from others. Many friends, family, and mentors are still here. Clients, managers, and teachers are still here. I believe you can create that legacy with your team and clients.

When you work with clients, and leave them with a solution, new product, new idea, or discussion piece, you are still here. When a past client gives you referrals, you are still here. When a person on your team implements a strategy that you helped him or her create, you are still here. As team members get promoted or move on to other opportunities and share what you have taught them, you are still here.

Part of this lesson could be to just *be here*. Be present. Put away distractions. Be focused on what is happening in front of you. The more you can *be* with the people and opportunities in front of you, the more opportunities you have to be here. Be willing to be here for others. We all rise when we lift others.

The other part is gratitude. Have appreciation for all those people and experiences that have shaped you. I think of my mom every day. Hopefully, you think about, and are grateful for, your own parents, siblings, teachers, mentors, coaches, and teammates who have taught you how to live. Have an attitude of gratitude. Be ready to pay forward all the wisdom that has been bestowed on you. Then, one day, you too can say, "I'm still here."

HE THAT SHALL PERSEVERE TO THE END, HE SHALL BE SAVED

52

LEADERSHIP

Santa Clara University (SCU) is a very special place to me. My grandfather, James Kennedy Carr, graduated from there in 1934 and was on the first Board of Regents. My mother, Ann Katherine Carr Dallosto, graduated in the first class of women in 1965 and served on the National Alumni Board. Growing up, we had many alumni events at our house. I only applied to one college and enrolled at SCU in the fall of 1989 as a business major.

During orientation, my mother was just beaming with excitement that I would share her joy and passion for Santa Clara. As we walked the grounds, we stopped in front of the Mission Santa Clara church because she wanted to show me something. The cross, from the original 1777 mission, is encased inside the current cross, which stands in front of the church. Across the top of the cross, the inscription reads, "He that shall persevere to the end, he shall be saved." My mom told me that when she was in school, she would say that prayer as she went by the cross before every test for good luck! There were many times in my four years at SCU that I did the same. It is still one of my favorite spots on campus and holds great sentimental value to me.

Perseverance is a great combination of persistence and commitment. When you are inspired to do what you do best, perseverance always pays off in the end. Whether you have been working toward a goal for ten minutes or ten years, your perseverance to see your vision to the end is what will save you. It will save you from setbacks, judgments, rejection, tight budgets, speed bumps, or a road block or two. Sometimes the best thing to do on a bad day is to take action to persevere toward the next day. That small sense of accomplishment in the light of daunting challenges can be the one thing that saves you. Persevere to the end. You will be saved.

SPECIAL THANKS

Special thanks to my love, Chuck Miller, who spent hours editing this book. Chuck is my foundation and the wind in my sails. Even though Chuck never met my mom, he honors her memory and has become a believer in her wisdom. Thank you also to our children for letting us share their stories and for their patience through this process.

My sister, Karolyn Pelka, helped start this process by writing down a lot of Mom's one-liners and sending me stories, too. Karolyn was often my sidekick when rolling our eyes at our mom's wisdom, but she too is now a believer and raises her children under the same backdrop of life lessons. My dad, Gene Dallosto, has been very supportive and willing to share some vulnerable moments. He was Mom's rock and constant support for 27 years, and a co-parent for 26 years. His contribution to our foundation is not highlighted, but without his steadiness and love, the wisdom may have been lost. Thanks, Dad!

Special thanks to my stepmother, Barbara Blair Dallosto. Barbara is a wonderful partner to my dad, and the only grandmother my kids have ever known. She gracefully supports us in honoring my mother's memory. Thank you for your grace and support, Barbara!

Thanks to all the teachers, administrators, professors, and principals who worked with Mom and those who were her students. The stories you have shared with me and with your students are a tribute to my mom and part of the legacy that she continues to have almost twenty years after her passing. Thank you for continuing to honor her through your stories.

These one-liners are a combination of quotes from my mom, dad, and others who have inspired me. They have helped me through relationships, divorce, child rearing, and a successful career. Everything comes with its ups and downs, these pearls of wisdom helped me along the way. Now I strive to help you as you go through your challenges and successes in life!

Grazie Mille,

Katey

ENDNOTES

1. Closed Mouths Don't Get Fed!
[1] *Glengarry Glen Ross*. DVD. Directed by James Foley. New Line Cinema, 1992.

3. If You Don't Want Anyone to Know It . . . Don't Do It
[1] Oprah.com. Online video. *The Powerful Lesson Maya Angelou Taught Oprah*. October 19, 2011. http://www.oprah.com/oprahs-lifeclass/the-powerful-lesson-maya-angelou-taught-oprah-video.
[2] Brown, Brené. *The Gifts of Imperfection: Let Go of Who You Think You're Supposed to Be and Embrace Who You Are*. Hazelden Publishing, 2010.

6. You Always Find What You Are Looking For
[1] Matthew 7:7-8. New International Version. Zondervan. 2011.

12. Life Doesn't Happen to You
[1] Ziglar, Zig. http://www.azquotes.com/quote/549167.

13. Vulnerability Creates Connection
[1] Brown, Brené. *The Power of Vulnerability*. Sounds True Publishing. 1994. https://www.ted.com/talks/brene_brown_on_vulnerability?language=en.
[2] Lencioni, Patrick. *The Five Dysfunctions of a Team*. Jossey-Bass. 2002. Page 196.

15. Don't Force It
[1] Osteen, Joel, *Your Best Life Now: Seven Steps to Living at Your Full Potential*. Faithwords, 2015. Page 203.

18. Champagne Emergency
[1] Keller Williams Realty national convention. Heard during a presentation. *Family Reunion*. 2009.

21. Tears Are Passion Manifested
[1] Valvano, Jimmy. "Jimmy's ESPY Awards Speech." www.jimmyv.org. March 4, 1993. https://www.jimmyv.org/about/remembering-jim/espy-awards-speech/.

22. If You Are Nice to People, You Get More Stuff

[1] Rossen, Jeff and Bomnin, Lindsey. "Rossen Report." www.today.com. June 9, 2016. http://www.today.com/money/score-freebies-your-vacation-simple-strategy-t96616.

23. It's All about the Fundamentals

[1] Lee, Bruce. https://www.brainyquote.com/quotes/quotes/b/brucelee413509.html.

[2] Lombardi, Vince. *Vince Lombardi on the Hidden Power of Mastering the Fundamentals*. March 01, 2017. http://www.huffingtonpost.com/james-clear/vince-lombardi-on-the-hid_b_9306782.html.

[3] Wooden, John. *John Wooden: First, How to Put on Your Socks*. October 24, 1999. http://www.newsweek.com/john-wooden-first-how-put-your-socks-167942.

[4] Duncan, Todd. *10 Steps to Build Your Pipeline & Close More Loans*. May 11. http://theduncangroup.com/blog/10-steps-to-build-your-pipeline-close-more-loans.

29. Agree to Disagree

[1] Lencioni, Patrick. *The Five Dysfunctions of a Team*. Jossey-Bass. 2002. Page 202.

31. The Best Salespeople Are from Chico State

[1] Maxwell, John C. *Failing Forward*. Thomas Nelson. 1982/2007. https://www.goodreads.com/work/quotes/614412-failing-forward-turning-mistakes-into-stepping-stones-for-success.

43. A Mentor's Hindsight Is Your Foresight

[1] The West Wing. Television show. Directed by Thomas Schlamme. (December 13, 2000; NBC). [In Episode #32 Noël, Leo tells Josh the following story . . .].

44. Be Comfortable Being Uncomfortable

[1] Unknown. *Struggle is Good! I Want to Fly!* http://instructor.mstc.edu/instructor/swallerm/Struggle%20-%20Butterfly.htm.

45. Go for No!

[1] Fenton, Richard and Waltz, Andrea. *Go for No!* Courage Crafters. 2007.

47. Compound Effect

[1] Hardy, Darren. *The Compound Effect*. Vanguard Press. 2010.

50. Friction Makes the Fire
[1] Lencioni, Patrick. *The Five Dysfunctions of a Team*. Jossey-Bass. 2002. Page 202.

51. I'm Still Here
[1] Anonymous. *To Those I Love and Those Who Love Me*. http://www.havenofnova.org/articles/poems/those_who_love_me.pdf

Electric Moon Publishing, LLC is an author-friendly, custom publishing place. EMoon collaborates with indie authors, ministries, organizations, and businesses in writing, editing, custom covers, specialty layouts, print, distribution, and marketing.

Visit us at www.emoonpublishing.com or contact us directly at info@emoonpublishing.com.